QUICK WINS!

Using Behavior Science to Accelerate and Sustain School Improvement

2ND EDITION

QUICK WINS!

Using Behavior Science to Accelerate and Sustain School Improvement

2ND EDITION

Paul Gavoni and Anika Costa

 KeyPress Publishing

KeyPress Publishing
www.keypresspublishing.com

KeyPress
Publishing

Authors: Paul Gavoni and Anika Costa

Quick Wins! Using Behavior Science to Accelerate and Sustain School Improvement (2nd ed.)

Published by: KeyPress Publishing
Publisher: Alice Darnell Lattal
Brand Integrity: Lisa Smith
Production Manager: Adele Hall
Editors: Ashley Johnson and Mary Sproles Martin
Designer: Jana Burtner

ISBN: 978-1-7377574-8-1

Distributed by:
ABA Technologies, Inc.
930 South Harbor City Blvd, Suite 402
Melbourne, FL 32901
www.abatechnologies.com

KeyPress Publishing books are available at a special discount for bulk purchases by corporations, institutions, and other organizations. For more information, please email keypress@abatechnologies.com.

TABLE OF CONTENTS

Acknowledgments

For most, writing a book is driven by passion, not profit. This is apropos as we both possess a deep passion for disseminating the science of human behavior across education to help make a positive difference. Between the two of us, we've spent more than 40 years working directly in or consulting with districts and schools. We love educators and truly believe they are the backbone of our nation. They deserve the greatest respect and should be provided the greatest support. We hope the content of the 2nd edition of *Quick Wins*, built from the teachings and mentoring of so many, continues to make a difference for them and the students they serve.

The concept of Quick Wins in education was originally formulated by Dr. Scott Neil circa 2010 as he led several turnarounds across Title I schools. Scott and Paul then collaborated, developed, and successfully applied the first system of Quick Wins. Paul then went on to work with Dr. Manuel "Manny" Rodriguez to refine and further operationalize this system and build the first version of *Quick Wins* (2016) on the principles of Organizational Behavior Management (OBM). To our knowledge, this was the first book dedicated to using OBM in schools.

We would like to extend our most sincere thanks to John Lynch for his 3+3+60=Trust strategy contribution to our book. In the story about the 3+3+60=Trust strategy, John is Principal Daniels. A former assistant superintendent, John is a remarkably accomplished turnaround principal who has transformed elementary, middle, and high schools. Also, sincere thanks to turnaround principal Jennifer Hedeen for her valuable contribution to the "Customer Service and Curbside Appeal" chapter.

We would like to thank our beloved families. We both feel remarkably fortunate to have "won the lottery" to have such caring and compassionate parents who have instilled values that perpetually drive us to respect and help others. Thank you to Susan and John Parry, Paul Gavoni, Annette Hawkins, and André Hawkins for molding us into who we are. This drive, fueled by our parents, is nurtured and further accelerated by our incredibly loving spouses Nikki Gavoni and Michael Costa, respectively, who regularly sacrifice to support our passion for bringing the science of human behavior to education. In your loving way, you each supply us with the courage and inspiration to push forward.

Last but not least, thank you to our children, Niko, Olivia, and Miles. Finding the words to describe how you have positively impacted us individually is difficult. So, we will dedicate this quote to you as it seems to sum it best up:

> *"While we try to teach our children all about life, our children teach us what life is all about."*
>
> – Angela Schwindt

There are many others who have supported us in our individual and collective journey. We'd likely have to write a separate book if we began naming you. You know who you are. We love you all and are grateful!

Paulie & Anika

Introduction

Thank you for picking up a copy of the 2nd edition of *Quick Wins*! This edition includes more chapters and more content, and is designed to provide an even better learning experience than the original. In this edition, you will find new and improved stories that help the reader better connect the dots; new and expanded examples of Quick Wins; a transition from traditional S.M.A.R.T. Goals to IMPACT Goals powered by behavior science; "Quick Takeaways" and "Sustain It" actions to extend the learning experience to actual improvements in schools; and much more!

SECTION I:

QUICK WINS

The book's goal is to be a school leader's "grab and go" resource for building momentum for change. Though it is written from the perspective of a school leader, you don't have to be a school leader to leverage the power of Quick Wins. Whether you are a school district official, principal, assistant principal, dean, guidance counselor, behavior analyst, or a school consultant, or you hold any administrative position where you engage people to implement change, this book is intended for you. Reading *Quick Wins* will give you a clear understanding and actionable steps related to:

- Engaging the team to rally around Quick Wins

- Using the power of direct observations and conversations during school improvement initiatives

- Understanding the importance of feedback to build trust, self-efficacy, and performance

- Perfecting the use and role of goals for school improvement

- Developing leadership's role in delivering effective communication and feedback

- Creating meaningful Quick Wins that can improve misbehavior, staff performance, and the school's climate and culture

CHAPTER 1

Hawkins Heights Elementary Fresh Paint and Targeted Misbehavior

"I can't take this anymore," the teacher sobbed, tears flowing down her face as chaos swirled around her.

Students ran up and down the hallway, laughing, pushing, and screaming toward the exit following the dismissal bell. "Today is my last day," she thought to herself. "I quit."

In the front office, there was chaos of another sort. There, students sat in the chairs lined up against the wall, whispering and giggling as angry parents surrounded the principal, hurling threats including: "I'm going to the district!" and "I'm taking my daughter out of this school."

"It's only November," the principal thought to himself in the middle of the barrage. "How will I make it to the end of this school year?"

The principal did make it to the end of the year. But Hawkins Heights Elementary's grade dropped from a C to an F. A climate survey sent out before the end of the year suggested that many faculty and staff planned on leaving. While the seasoned principal had been leading schools for years, this was his first year as an administrator in a school located in an area characterized by high crime and poverty. He didn't feel he could make a difference or meet the demands of the school. After considering the situation and his fate, he decided to quit.

Now, district leadership needed a principal for Hawkins Heights Elementary for the upcoming school year. They wanted someone who could turn the school around. Immediately, they thought of Augustus Daniels, an experienced principal with a track record of turning around failing schools. "We need your help," the district pleaded. "More importantly, the students, faculty, and staff need your help."

As the leaders made their case to Principal Daniels, he thought about the school. He was familiar with it. Besides regularly hearing rumors of numerous challenges at the school, he recalled that the district had hosted training for him and a group of other principals earlier in the school year at Hawkins Heights. He remembers several issues he observed while visiting the school. The congested traffic getting into the school's parking lot had kept him from his usual practice of arriving early. Then there was the overgrown grass skirting faded walls blotched with rust stains from the sprinkler. As he headed to the front office, he noted there seemed to be very few faculty and staff in the hallways. As such, he wasn't surprised to see students running past him, laughing, yelling, and pushing as they headed toward the chaotic cafeteria for breakfast. Student work and signs of school pride were absent on the hallway walls. He recalled standing in the front office patiently waiting for anyone to acknowledge his presence so he could ask where to sign in.

Most of all, he remembered leaving the school that day exhausted from his experience. He felt concerned for the students, faculty, and staff. And though he knew this was a leadership issue, he felt bad for the principal and his leadership team. They seemed to be good people with good intentions. They just didn't know what they didn't know.

With all this in mind, Principal Daniels agreed to take over at Hawkins Heights. The impoverished elementary school was characterized by low achievement and a high frequency of misbehavior. Parents were disillusioned with the school and demanded change. He knew the faculty and staff struggled daily, burdened with the pressure to improve, and that this left them highly motivated to pursue greener pastures at other schools.

The district, wanting to avoid losing faculty and staff familiar with the students and the community, met with them during the last week of school to announce that Principal Daniels would be taking over the next year. The district knew he had a good reputation. And their strategy paid off as many faculty and staff decided to stay to see what this new principal could offer.

Recognizing that he was under a microscope, Principal Daniels knew he must do something fast to strengthen faculty and staff belief in his vision and to motivate them to engage in any change initiative. Not only did he want everyone to believe in his vision—he needed his faculty and staff to believe in themselves. He also wanted them to believe that actual change was at hand.

His first action, taken before their first day back at school, was to have the school freshly painted. He felt it was important for everybody to see an immediate positive change. Principal Daniels greeted the members of his school at the front door that first day back and welcomed them into the meeting space. When the faculty and staff returned to the school from summer break, they immediately noticed the fresh paint. As they arrived, many commented on how good the school looked and that they liked the chosen paint color.

As the teachers and staff funneled into the media center and took their seats, the room felt different. Principal Daniels noted the smiles and the chatter about the changes in the school as he circled the space. He called them to start the meeting by sounding a delightful chime. The adults finished their conversations, grabbed their last bagels, pastries, and cups of coffee from the spread provided, and quickly took their seats. Principal Daniels opened the meeting by posing a question: "I want you to think about your values and what's important to you. Also, I'd like to know what changes you would like to see in the school. Use a whiteboard to write down your responses, and after a few minutes, we'll share our thoughts."

The faculty and staff were very candid with their responses. They had not been asked questions like that before, and it seemed as though Principal Daniels was very open to hearing what they had to say. They said, "We can't teach like we want to. There are so many behavior issues across the campus. We don't feel we can discipline the students; what are we supposed to do when they misbehave?" A major theme that emerged during the meeting was that the school needed a plan to reduce misbehavior incidents.

After hearing their concerns, Principal Daniels interviewed some parents and students to get their input. The parents, in particular, were upset about what they saw when dropping their children off and picking them up from school. "It seems like the Wild West around here," one parent reflected. And another reported, "My daughter usually takes the bus to school. But last year, I had to bring her to school a few times following a doctor's appointment. When I signed her in at the front office, nobody smiled or said good morning to either of us. They just looked like they didn't want to be there." That was certainly consistent with Principal Daniels's experience the previous school year.

After conducting more interviews and reviewing other existing data, Principal Daniels asked for input from faculty and staff to set an initial goal for improving three areas: (1) student behavior when arriving at school, (2) student behavior at lunchtime in the cafeteria, and (3) staff behavior and attitude in the front office. He knew that though there were many other issues, if everything was important, then nothing was important. The first two focus areas of arrival and lunchtime were determined to be fertile grounds for misbehavior and where his staff struggled most to handle it. He also knew that arrival time was the first thing students, faculty, staff, parents, and the community experienced on any given day. Just as the fresh coat of paint and hallway decorations were the first things the faculty and staff noticed right away when they walked into the building after the summer break. Similarly, while not as visible to parents and the community, the cafeteria was a common area and the behavior there was highly visible and regularly experienced by the stakeholders at school.

Though many teachers complained of misbehavior in the classroom, this was a larger hurdle to overcome, and the teachers seemed doubtful that the principal could improve these issues. Consequently, he believed that lunch and arrival times could be immediately transformed in a way that would also positively impact behavior in the classroom. He reasoned that behavior in the classroom should improve as students would be more likely to enter a class calmly and ready to learn. And as far as the front office staff, they were essentially the face of the school. Their interactions with the parents, students, faculty, and staff were important to the climate and culture of the school. They were also a critical part of the arrival time for everyone who entered the school. In addition, Principal Daniels knew that if he wanted buy-in from the stakeholders to take on more and bigger challenges associated with student achievement, he would need them to believe in him and themselves.

To initiate this change, Principal Daniels and his leadership team provided brief training to the faculty and staff who supervised the cafeteria and arrivals—training on teaching and reinforcing expectations and specific corrective procedures to follow when misbehavior occurred. Similarly, he met with the front desk staff to discuss the importance of their roles to the school's success, then delivered a brief in-service on providing customer satisfaction.

Following the training, the principal asked his leadership team to keep their schedules open during arrival and lunchtime. The leadership team's role was three-fold: (1) walk around—be present; (2) engage with the staff managing these situations; and (3) thank staff for being at their post, praising any positive interactions observed during these times, including interactions in the front office.

If misbehavior occurred, the principal asked the leadership team not to intervene with students directly but to coach the staff on the specific corrective procedures taught during the training. Once the leadership team completed the coaching, the leader would request the staff to apply these strategies while the leader observed. If the staff applied the strategies effectively, the leader was to praise the correct implementation of the strategies and point out the impact of these strategies on student behavior.

As the school year started, the principal began observing these areas and noticed when the students ran in the hallways during arrival time; they were told to "walk" by the attending staff. As part of Principal Daniels's plan, staff no longer said, "Walk." Instead, they were to say, "Walk back to where you began running." And then, as they walked by again, the staff would smile and say, "Thanks for walking. Have a great day!" This strategy, called positive practice, slightly delayed the student attempting to transition somewhere fast. In the future, to avoid this delay, those students who had typically run began walking. Besides positively correcting the students' behavior who had been running, other students vicariously learned that running would result in having to walk back. Within 1 week, the difference in the students' hallway behavior was visible to staff, but also to parents and district personnel who supported the school and were shocked at the obvious change.

After the first week of implementing the new strategies, the principal decided to compare his new discipline data to previous years. To his pleasant surprise, there had been an 80% reduction in discipline referrals during the first hour of school, a fact he immediately shared and celebrated with the faculty, staff, and leadership team, acknowledging their hard work in producing this result. After 2 weeks, the principal met with his leadership team to assess and target a few more areas for a quick change that would positively and visibly impact faculty, staff, and student behaviors. They then systematically used this strategy throughout the year as each goal was met.

At the end of his first year, this principal had moved his school three letter grades, from an F to a B. Staff morale and retention were the highest in the district, and parents and district administrators praised the school for their amazing turn-around. Principal Daniels was confident they would be an A school the next year.

How could some paint and a few simple protocols in common areas have such an impact on student achievement, retention, and morale? Two words: Quick Wins! Quick Wins are science-based and replicable rocket fuel for school leaders to propel change and transformation initiatives beyond the "gravity" that prevented previous initiatives from launching.

The Reason Leaders Struggle to Change Schools

One of the primary goals of any public school system is to equip students with the knowledge and skills that will allow them to become college and career ready. An effective school increases a student's chances of achievement and thus propels the student toward that goal (Marzano et al., 2009). Investigations have cited many reasons why schools have not successfully achieved desired results. Several researchers have suggested that ineffective teacher preparation programs (Eckert, 2013) have led to insufficient and even counterproductive district, leadership, and teacher behavior (Marzano et al., 2005; Marzano & Waters, 2009) that have hurt student achievement. As a result, many people have begun pointing their fingers. And that just makes things worse. As behaviorists, our belief echoes the writings of Dr. B. F. Skinner in his article "The Shame of American Education" (1984):

1. Students who fail have not been taught.

2. Teachers who provide poor instruction have not been prepared.

3. Teacher preparation programs have not been required to infuse the science of behavior into their instructional programs.

The hard fact is that too many educators are entering schools unprepared to meet the demands of an ever-changing environment. This under-preparedness leaves district leaders in a predicament as resources are typically stretched to the limit; moreover, it forces school leaders to continuously adapt as conditions shift in a sometimes-turbulent economy and evolving society. To lead school improvement, leadership must develop a plan to promote a systematic effort to move faculty and staff behavior toward change initiatives. This plan will require school leaders to promote a strong vision that motivates them and their team to implement the strategies for targeted goals. Change needs to be managed effectively by the school leaders and their team as patterns are assessed and problems are solved through collaborative efforts.

Managing change effectively can be complex depending on factors including the size of the change and the size of the school (Hall & Hord, 2011). Too often, change management techniques are misguided in their strategy and approach—exacerbating the problem. In these cases, school leaders create mandates, change vision, and make different requests of faculty and staff but they leave out strategies for initiating the change and managing human performance, all of which comprise the situation, behaviors, tasks, and results (Daniels & Daniels, 2006). Whether it be improving student achievement or behavior, educator performance is critical for this change to occur (Owens & Valesky, 2015). Although mandates will work, Hall and Hord (2011) suggest that mandate strategies will fail "when the only time the change process is supported is at the initial announcement of the mandate" (p. 15).

While creating a strong vision can—and will—inspire change (Cornish, 2004), focusing on telling faculty and staff what they should do without examining how their daily behaviors are changing is not enough. A common approach for managing change starts and ends with a school leader making a great speech about the new vision and direction at the beginning of a change innovation. These leaders fail to gain buy-in or embed a performance management system to shape the transformation process. In short, when change initiatives fail, it is typically a result of a failure to engage the participation of the stakeholders and put in place contingencies that will support the behaviors necessary for success. All results require behavioral changes. And leading school improvement requires people to change their behavior. It's all about behavior! As such, having a fundamental understanding of the science of human behavior through Quick Win strategies can help school leaders effectively initiate and maintain sustainable change.

Whether it be asked of a district, school, classroom, teacher, or student, change is often hard for those involved as it requires engaging in new behaviors. Many people resist change, whether it is small or large. Unfortunately, this resistance often stalls transformation, leaving school leaders scratching their heads as they reflect on a year's worth of struggle with little to show. Had many of these leaders possessed *Quick Wins* strategies for building behavioral momentum, like Principal Daniels, they likely would have accelerated change initiatives and met or even exceeded achievement goals. But what are Quick Wins?

A Quick Win is a visible improvement that can be delivered quickly with immediate benefits. People want to see meaningful improvement—and they want to see it quickly. Like Hawkins Heights Elementary, these improvements are easily identifiable, as they could have, and should have, been made long ago. A Quick Win does not have to be profound or have a long-term impact on your school. However, the best Quick Wins are long-lasting and leave a profound effect on faculty and staff's interest and ability to make long-term-impact changes happen. One thing is certain: A Quick Win necessitates that people agree on the need for change, act together to make the change, and learn from the change. To make such change happen, Quick Wins require leadership.

A Quick Win is a leader-led approach. School transformation, or any other large-scale change, relies on the specific behaviors of the leader.

School leaders must empower others to establish a culture where people embrace and implement change. The need for school turnaround and the current struggles that are overwhelmingly common within the process both require school leaders to take an active role. Considering the common failures in school turnarounds and their root causes, leadership's role in launching any change becomes critical.

Our driving philosophies and practices in *Quick Wins* are grounded in deep experience in applying the science of human behavior in the workplace. This is formally known as Organizational Behavior Management (OBM). OBM applies a blend of applications, such as social learning theory, applied behavior analysis, and business management techniques, to create the very core of *Quick Wins*. These foundations support our contention of leadership's role in creating a positive climate and culture for building and sustaining school transformation.

Quick Wins are not gimmicks, flavors of the month, or silver bullets. Quick Wins give you the critical building blocks for rapidly accelerating change by providing a platform for leaders to build upon. Quick Wins are based on science and apply evidence-based approaches to make change happen and last.

As the Quick Wins approach is leader-led, before we teach you how to identify Quick Wins, we will first dig into the concept of leadership in the following chapters. Moving forward, we will interchangeably use terms such as *school transformation, school turnaround, school improvement,* and *change initiatives.* The reason being that whatever you term the process, they all have the same things in common: behavior and results.

Quick Takeaways:

- Quick Wins are visible improvements that have immediate benefits and can be delivered quickly. They are rooted in science, applying evidence-based approaches to making change happen and last.

- Quick Wins can be leveraged by anybody supporting schools.

- To lead school improvement, a plan must be developed to promote a systematic effort to move faculty and staff behavior toward change initiatives.

- All results require changes in behavior. Leading and school improvement, climate or culture shift require people to do something more, less, or differently to change their behavior.

- Quick Wins are a leader-led approach that require the leader to involve the stakeholders in the change process.

Sustain It:

- How might you involve the stakeholders in change initiatives at your school. What specific examples can you identify?

- Reflect on change initiatives for your school. What might you identify as Quick Wins?

- What are some ways you, as a leader, can address the lack of teacher preparedness? How might you support teachers? Identify some resources that can help.

CHAPTER 2:

Quick Wins Require Leadership

It is important to understand that every school has its own culture or personality. Some might expand that to "personality disorder!" Each school requires a customized approach to achieving the desired improvement or transformation. And this is why a "one-size fixes all" approach just won't work. At Hawkins Heights Elementary, the previous principal failed to replicate what he did at his other school. Even though he was a seasoned principal who maintained good outcomes, those same approaches didn't work for Hawkins Heights. Principal Daniels was successful because he listened to the stakeholders and identified their needs. Their trouble spots or pain points were unique to their school.

However, there *is* one constant in all turnaround efforts. It is the constant that differentiates successful turnarounds from failures. It gets highlighted in the media and talked about by parents and teachers alike. It truly sets the tone of the school turnaround process from the start. This constant is *leadership*!

According to Marzano et al. (2005), "A highly effective school leader can have a dramatic influence on the overall academic achievement of students" (p. 97). In one study, the researchers found a 0.25 correlation between the leadership behavior of the school's principal and the average academic achievement; furthermore, researchers found that principals who were one standard deviation beyond the average in terms of leadership skills could raise student achievement by as much as 34%. Notice that this is just one person: the school leader.

School turnarounds require sound leadership action to motivate people to accelerate change rapidly. What a school leader does to make such changes happen depends on the school's specific needs: Are students failing? Are teachers quitting? Is the building in disrepair? Is the school under-enrolled, leaving the district wondering if it should be shut down? Are leaders feeling unsupported by their district leaders?

Unfortunately, in most turnaround cases, there is not just one problem. This reality drives many school leaders to try changing everything at once. This approach leads nowhere fast. We agree with Simon Sinek, leadership consultant and best-selling author of the book, *Start with Why: How Great Leaders Inspire Everyone to Take Action* (2009) who suggests, "It is better to go slow in the right direction than to go fast in the wrong direction" (Sinek, 2021).

In the first year of a turnaround, teachers leave without any observable positive changes, and stakeholders quickly question the leadership because there is insufficient support for any initiatives to develop a successful trend. Under these conditions, a few outcomes are almost certain: The leader is asked to leave, the school fails, and, most importantly, the students fall short of their potential.

In contrast to trying to do it all, Quick Wins are about taking a focused, carefully targeted stance to support a few key areas to make a visible change happen and stick.

With these successes, leaders earn trust, buy-in, and establish a track record to engage in further change. The leader benefits in implementing Quick Wins by developing self-efficacy, which is belief in one's own ability to complete a task and in one's response efficacy—in other words, belief in one's ability to produce an outcome successfully. These concepts are important because faculty and staff must reach goals confidently. A critical leadership approach requires regular measurement and effective feedback. The *Quick Wins* approach creates a strong foundation for the future, enabling leaders to achieve success along the way to school transformation.

Leading and Managing

Regardless of the setting, influence is the root of the most effective leadership. But it requires a very particular type of influence: Managers hold people accountable, and leaders inspire people to feel responsible for their behavior and outcomes (Geller, 2003).

Like peanut butter and jelly, leadership and management are complementary and are typically required for the regular pursuit and accomplishment of short- and long-term goals—especially in education. School leaders must regularly engage in leading, managing, training, and coaching behaviors, as each has specific purposes or functions.

Effective leading is about building and strengthening relationships, facilitating self-accountability, and using feedback to make progress toward goal attainment a source of value and reinforcement. Effective management is about facilitating order and establishing consistency and accountability using performance feedback to let people know where they stand concerning goals and what they can do to move closer to them (Balcazar et al., 1985-1986).

Where leading is about outlining a path and getting people to move in the right direction collectively, managing is about coordinating and ensuring individual members of staff or faculty stay on course. Daniels and Daniels (2007) suggest that the durability of a leader's vision depends on the quality of management. The leader, therefore, needs to be involved in management as much as necessary to ensure systems and processes are in place. At times this may require "managing the managers." In the school setting, this might mean managing members of the school leadership team or faculty in their efforts toward managing the students. In the end, the school leader should be primarily a source of inspiration, but what exactly is inspiration?

While inspiration might be thought of as short-term motivation to behave toward a goal, if educators or students continue performing toward that goal, they must find continued meaning in the task and outcome. Whether at the district, school, or classroom level, the best educational leaders know this and can inspire what they often call "intrinsic" motivation.

Intrinsic Motivation

First of all, intrinsic motivation probably "ain't whatcha think"! To the behavioral layperson, intrinsic motivation is behavior driven by internal rewards. In other words, the motivation to engage in a behavior, such as those associated with school improvement, arises within the individual because it is naturally satisfying. Most people think it comes from inside you. And that's understandable. When you do something you "want" to do ... well, you can essentially "feel" that want inside you. And that want inside of you can evoke certain behaviors to help you satisfy that "want," right? The fact that we have bodily sensations that we "tact" or label as emotions, feelings, etc., is not debatable. We all experience these private events that we can observe but others can't. But let's think about "intrinsic" motivation. What is that you want? What satisfies that itch? Is it something inside you? Or is it the act of doing something and its positive outcomes that help you feel satisfied?

If you pick up a book, read and enjoy it, the source of your satisfaction is within the book. In other words, the satisfaction is "intrinsic" to the task itself (reading), not within yourself. Each word and sentence you read engages you and makes you desire to keep reading more. For students who love math, each time they solve a math problem, they are "rewarded" for engaging successfully in solving the problem. Conversely, if they don't perform it correctly, they desire to correct it. Just as different people enjoy different flavors of ice cream, reading, and math can be "naturally" satisfying to a particular individual. That's why they may continue to read the books they enjoy or solve math problems they find challenging even when nobody is telling them to do so.

Motivation is often found *within the task itself* that drives the person's behavior. We can also call that *reinforcement*. But what exactly is reinforcement? Reinforcement involves consequences that strengthen behavior or increase the likelihood that a given behavior will occur again. For example, when you first experienced a headache, it was probably suggested you take some medication such as aspirin to remove the pain. If taking the aspirin worked for you and alleviated your pain, there's a good chance you will continue to seek and take aspirin each time you have a headache.

Whether it be the aspirin-taking or reading a book or completing math problems, all are examples of reinforcement as the behaviors reoccurred. Similarly, the behavior is rewarded in these cases because of the reinforcement it produces. In other words, nobody had to tell the person engaging in those behaviors they were doing a great job. In each case, the reinforcement or intrinsic motivation was inherent to the task. Behaviorally speaking, intrinsic motivation can be thought of as changes in stimulation produced by the behavior itself (Horcones, 1983) or what is known as automatic reinforcement. This contrasts "external" motivation or reinforcement found outside or "extra" to the task itself. For example, becoming a school leader solely for financial gain instead of the personal satisfaction of helping students achieve is based on external motivation.

Most behavior is under a confluence of both "intrinsic" and "extrinsic" motivation. It occurs because of the different reinforcers it produces that are idiosyncratic to the person. For Principal Daniels, there were likely multiple sources of reinforcement (motivation) including financial gain, the satisfaction of helping faculty perform well and seeing students succeed, perhaps the positive feedback received from district leaders and the community, and more. All these *added* outcomes associated with leadership are considered positive reinforcement if they keep leadership behavior going.

In the behavior sciences, positive and negative terms are not value statements. They simply mean that behavior continues because something is *added* or *subtracted* as a result of it. Positive reinforcement, as in the examples of reading and math, brings forth discretionary effort (Lattal & Porritt, 2008), as evidenced by people going above and beyond to produce that reinforcement, even when nobody is looking.

In many cases, avoiding a penalty (the school leader wants to avoid losing funding) or removing something unwanted (easing a headache by taking an aspirin) might also be thrown into the mix as a source of motivation. This serves as a source of negative reinforcement as the school leader also behaves to *subtract* or avoid undesirable consequences.

While negative reinforcement is a part of personal and professional life, it has a ceiling that can be characterized as compliance. When people are driven by negative reinforcement, they will do just enough to get by or to avoid that "unwanted" something by ensuring they are in "compliance." Think about it. In the aspirin example, people only take enough aspirin to get rid of the headache. When it comes to paying bills, most people pay just enough to avoid late fees. Unfortunately, too many leaders in any role or industry attempt to leverage this reinforcement through fear of unwanted consequences to drive employee behavior. Or, in the case of the classroom leader, to drive student behavior.

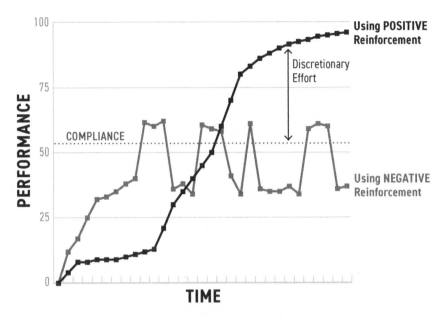

FIGURE 2.1: Negative reinforcement, or fear of consequences, generates compliance (at best) at the expense of many other things. Getting people to go above and beyond (discretionary effort) requires positive reinforcement. Adapted from Lattal and Porritt (2008).

Negative reinforcement does move behavior forward; however, as clearly illustrated in the graph above (Lattal & Porritt, 2008), it typically results in compliance (at best), low morale, high turnover, lack of innovation, and a myriad of other outcomes associated with the regular use of negative reinforcement to drive behavior. And when used to drive student behavior, it usually results in more behavioral challenges and less student achievement. In education, it is the school leader who sets the tone for the use of positive reinforcement versus negative reinforcement. In other words, if the principal regularly uses fear of consequences or negative reinforcement to drive educator behavior, there is a good chance it will adversely affect faculty and staff performance. It may also increase the likelihood that the faculty and staff will use the same strategies or negative reinforcement modeled by the school leader in their interactions with students.

Measuring Educational Leadership

The greatest school leaders in history have helped people find meaning in their day-to-day tasks. In other words, they fostered motivational effects by helping faculty and staff—and, in the case of the classroom leader, students—experience the task as positive reinforcement. Though the day-to-day task might be mundane, completing it lets them know they are contributing to something bigger, which serves as a source of satisfaction (i.e., positive reinforcement).

While it's extremely hard to determine just how much a school or classroom leader is arranging conditions that increase staff/student motivation, in their book *Measure of a Leader*, Aubrey Daniels and James Daniels (2007) outline some simple metrics that can be used as indicators of a school leader's positive influence. Check out the questions below. They are designed to gauge motivation. The more "yes" responses to these questions, the more likely the leader is to foster discretionary effort, going above and beyond the expected.

1. Do you put any extra effort into their initiatives?

2. When the school leader asks you to do something, do you start immediately?

3. Are you working now on their top priority issues?

4. Do you see the connection between your daily efforts and the school leader's vision?

5. Can you cite an example of another faculty or staff living the school leader's values?

6. Do you invest as much energy and enthusiasm as the school leader invests into his/her initiatives?

7. Can you give a recent example where a peer has helped you with your work?

8. Do other departments or grade groups cooperate and assist your department or grade group?

9. How many suggestions for improvement have you made to the school leader within the last 3 months?

10. Is it safe to admit to the school leader that you have made a mistake or failed at something?

11. Is the school leader someone you would respect for counsel and advice?

12. Does the school leader actively encourage you to improve your skills and personal growth?

Ultimately, it does matter how motivation is defined. Think of motivation as residing in the conditions that surround us. The point is the more a school leader provides an environment of positive involvement, the more faculty and staff find value in undertaking tasks related to school improvement goals, and the more likely they will strive to achieve those goals, even when the school leader is not looking. One of the essential functions of Quick Wins is getting faculty and staff in touch with valued outcomes as quickly and efficiently as possible. This means getting them in touch with positive reinforcement.

Vision, Mission, and Value Statements Aren't Leading

It's not unusual for school leaders to spend a lot of time and other resources developing vision, mission, and value statements. Yet if you ask the faculty and staff, you'd find it a challenge to locate many people who know what these are; more importantly, you would likely find it hard to distinguish consistent behaviors that espouse the beautifully written vision and mission, and values. Values are intended to guide tasks, processes, and systems linked to the school's mission that will eventually lead to the vision, or what Jim Collins and Jerry Porras (1997) call a "Big Hairy Audacious Goal" (p. 10).

Now, at the root of the accomplishment of any goal (including a Quick Win) the basic unit of analysis is behavior. As we said before, it all boils down to behavior. In a school, it is the collective behavior—or habits—of everyone that makes up that culture or "the way we do things around here." And it is the collective perception of everyone that makes up the school's climate, or "how we feel about the way we do things around here." Similarly, your collective behaviors and often the perception of your behaviors' outcomes characterize your leadership and how you feel about it. What you do and what happens as a result will influence how you think, feel, and behave in the future. In other words, it will influence your self-efficacy and response-efficacy. Moreover, it will influence how the faculty, staff, and students think, feel, and behave in the future, or their collective self- and response-efficacy.

The moment-to-moment, day-to-day, and week-to-week behaviors make or break you as a school leader. Each behavior in and of itself may not seem a big deal, but the aggregate of these behaviors drives achievement—or failure to achieve. Developing value statements is an important part of the process, especially when such statements guide leadership behavior. But simply writing or talking about values will not necessarily lead you or your school to engage in valued and ethical behavior. Nor will it achieve Quick Wins. These require collective behavior change.

While people might write this or say that, it turns out that writing this and saying that does not reliably predict behavior, no matter your role in education. According to Daniels and Daniels (2007), "Talk is valuable for clarifying examples and non-examples of ethical conduct, but for most people, the conversation does not lead to behavior change" (p. 75). You see, talk and value statements are typically antecedent strategies. Antecedents are much like instructions or reminders that help get behavior going. While antecedents can serve as motivation to get behavior moving in the right direction (like a road map, in this case), the consequences, or reinforcement, result from those behaviors that ensure it will continue. As you have learned, without reinforcement, there is no change in behavior!

Getting people to behave in ways aligned with the school's values takes far more than good statements. In the most effective schools we've observed, the process starts at the top, whereby the school's leadership team models and reinforces valued behavior. First, modeling valued behavior increases the likelihood that a school's faculty, staff, and students will engage in that behavior. When this occurs, the school's leadership team is in a position to positively reinforce. When faculty, staff, and students consistently experience value (i.e., reinforcement or meaningful consequences) due to their behavior, they will likely engage in that behavior again and again. This value-added behavior moves you toward Quick Wins and positive outcomes. And when their peers see valuable consequences, it increases the likelihood they will engage in similar behaviors. Consider the teacher struggling with transitioning her students who observes a colleague using a specific strategy to line up the students successfully. If she sees the students lining up efficiently and orderly, she is likely to adopt the same strategy. As more faculty, staff, and students engage in value-added behavior, this simultaneously increases the opportunity for the school leadership team to reinforce that behavior positively. In cultures like this, reinforcement begins to flow in all directions—up, down, and laterally—as it becomes embedded in the school's culture.

What are some of the day-to-day examples of positive reinforcement? If a school leader values the cooperation of her faculty and staff, she would include them in decision-making—as Principal Daniels did when he involved the stakeholders in the turnaround efforts at Hawkins Heights. To improve or maintain performance, the school leader may use behavior-specific praise, telling the faculty and staff exactly what they are doing well. This could be in the form of the faculty and staff receiving individual, group, or schoolwide feedback regularly from the school leader, letting the stakeholders know what leadership liked about their behavior and also discussing the outcomes of their behavior as it relates to school improvement goals. In this way, faculty and staff can link their behavior to important accomplishments and results.

Imagine a leadership team increasing the use of positive reinforcement for desired behaviors. Eventually, faculty and staff might begin delivering positive reinforcement for appropriate student behavior. The result cascades positive reinforcement of valued behavior aligned with key accomplishments and school improvement goals. For this to occur, core systems rooted in positive reinforcement must be in place. Some examples include:

- Recognizing and praising incremental improvement in critical instructional behavior

- Leaving positive feedback daily via emails and sticky notes left on teachers' desks

- Spinning "wheels of fortune" that are packed with a variety of inexpensive tokens of appreciation

With core systems grounded in positive reinforcement, one would be hard pressed to find much at a principal's school that was not intended to help faculty and staff grow, to value their work, value the learning, and value the school's mission. Even in struggling schools, when the principal focuses on leveraging positive reinforcement to help faculty and staff grow and accomplish their goals, it is not long before the faculty and staff can shift their focus toward helping the students grow and achieve their goals.

In any school, it is very clear that this multiplier effect occurs when leaders model and reinforce valued and ethical behavior. Similarly, when school leaders treat their faculty and staff well and establish themselves as positive reinforcers, like behavioral karma (DiNovi & Gavoni, 2021), good things return to them. Unfortunately, too often, school leaders either miss or fail to capitalize on a grand opportunity for developing or strengthening valued behavior, simply because the school's values tend only to be discussed following a violation of some rule. This happens in the classroom, too. For example, a teacher talks to students only when they violate some rule but fails to recognize all the good things they do in their day-to-day activities. While correcting the behavior of students (or even of faculty and staff) might result in them avoiding the particular behavior that resulted in a rule violation, it doesn't ensure they will engage in what is truly valued. Too often, they might be scolded or told what *not* to do but not taught *how* to do, nor reinforced for doing, what is truly important. School and classroom leaders who recognize and make positive examples of those displaying behaviors representative of the values supported by the school are far more likely to strengthen good habits and create a value-driven culture. If these habits are linked to the critical accomplishments and school improvement goals driven by the mission, the school is very likely to achieve powerful Quick Wins and sustainable results.

People First, Programs Second

Richard Branson, the famed entrepreneur and owner of Virgin Airlines, is widely quoted as saying, "Clients do not come first. Employees come first. If you take care of the employees, they will take care of the clients." It is surprising how many district and school leaders don't understand that people—employees—come before programs!

If education aims to bring out the best in its students, leaders must bring out the best in the teachers and staff who impact student achievement. The school community needs to be involved in the turnaround process from day one. People don't want things "done to them." This leads to people working in compliance mode and doing the bare minimum to keep others happy and avoid getting into trouble.

The most successful school leaders we have worked with understand that all stakeholders within a school community need to have their voices heard on how to proceed with any significant change initiative. Building teamwork and shared responsibility toward solving the various challenges of turning around a school fosters collaboration and strengthens relationships amongst the staff in ways that produce results for many more years than any single program could. An invested staff will propel leadership much farther toward sustainable change than will throwing dollars toward the latest technology program or curriculum that is supposed to fix everything.

It's all about trust. Programs will go nowhere if they lack staff buy-in and a sense of purpose. Effective school leaders develop relationships built on mutual trust between themselves and the rest of the school community. Trust is not some mystical phenomenon requiring yearly trust-building exercises. Good school leaders who follow through on what they say are trusted.

Trust is essential for solidifying the development of strong relationships; in addition to trusting in the school leader, people who do not feel trusted *by* the leader will be less than willing to provide the extra effort it takes to make the school a place of high achievement for all.

Schools where faculty and staff lack trust will have employees who focus on doing just enough to get by. Some will even sabotage efforts and negatively impact a school's sense of connectedness and drive to become great. Building relationships built on trust is a powerful way for school leaders to establish themselves as positive reinforcers and powerful sources of motivation.

Quick Takeaways:

- Intrinsic motivation is a common term for the motivation that drives the person's behavior. It is assumed most often to be something inside the person. We define it as in reality being found within the tasks and activities of daily life that surround us, not inside the person. People going above and beyond their daily tasks when no one is looking are exhibiting behavior that has been highly reinforced by the motivational effects of the settings they find themselves in.

- Reinforcement strengthens behavior and increases the likelihood that the behavior will occur again in the future.

- Getting people to behave in ways that align with the school's vision, mission, and values requires modeling and reinforcement of valued behavior by the leadership.

Sustain It:

- Think about how often you deliver positive reinforcement to your stakeholders. What specific examples can you identify?

- Change initiatives will only go somewhere when stakeholders are involved. What are some ways to include stakeholders to get buy-in?

- Trust is essential for solidifying the development of solid relationships. Think of some ways you might build trust with your stakeholders. Reflect on them.

CHAPTER 3:

Quick Wins Require Positive and Systematic Leadership

No Quick Win will work without leadership. As you've surmised, the defining characteristic of successful schools is leadership that leverages positive reinforcement. Why faculty and staff stay in or leave schools usually comes down to leadership. Not surprisingly, active, proactive, engaging, positive leadership makes Quick Wins successful during a school's turnaround. In other words, real leadership is influencing others *toward a positive outcome.*

Without this critical positive element in leadership, one could describe Adolf Hitler, Genghis Kahn, and Saddam Hussein as great leaders! Each influenced others and was followed by many. However, their leadership resulted in horrible acts of violence and oppression, ruling others without regard for consequences and punishing those who defied them.

Such leadership has no place in education—or anywhere for that matter— and thus we use this definition: Leadership is influencing others to achieve a positive outcome with them.

Characteristics of Positive Leadership

The characteristics of positive leadership have been researched extensively. In 2015, Krapfl and Kruja wrote for the *Journal of Organizational Behavior Management* a list of common leader characteristics that support a successful school turnaround. We summarize nine here to provide content and context as we link these characteristics to the turnaround experience.

 I. **LEADERS PROVIDE A VALUE PROPOSITION:** Similar to a vision, where the school leader specifies a desired future state, a value proposition identifies the relationship between the school and the larger context the school serves. What is our value proposition as educators? It is to provide excellent education to produce the next generation of scientists, writers, business-people, and, generally speaking, contributors to society.

As Krapfl and Kruja (2015) share, when leading an organization in a new direction, "if the value proposition is not strong, the effort will ultimately fail" (p. 32). During a school turnaround, a leader can provide such a value proposition to the educators teaching the students, the parents of the students, and the external community. The school can turn around, and everyone wins once the turnaround is complete. That's the value.

2. **LEADERS SHOW ETHICAL VALUES:** Leaders must be ethical. They must demonstrate high integrity to earn the trust of their followers. In the educational system, this is essential. Leaders who do not have the trust of their people can and will fail in the long run, regardless of Quick Wins. These ethical values create confidence, demand for success, and long-term viability for the school.

3. **LEADERS DEMONSTRATE EXECUTION SKILLS:** Our focus on Quick Wins is about executing strategies that will positively impact the school during a tough time. Unfortunately, this is an abundant challenge: Execution typically needs to be taught in school, and execution skills often need to be improved in leaders of organizations, whether business or educational. Many school leaders make the mistake of assuming that once everyone understands the plan, the implementation is simple. Nothing is further from the truth! Plans do not turn into actions automatically. Plans demand leadership to make things happen, to engage people to implement the plans to make a difference. Leaders can learn execution skills and should learn from their peers, from mentors, and through formal higher education.

4. **LEADERS ENCOURAGE INNOVATION AND CREATIVITY:** An effective leader engages people to be innovative and creative, especially during a turnaround. With innovation and creativity, morale can be high, and results can continue or be achievable. A turnaround is a special challenge for a new school leader because the faculty and staff have a history with the school that might lead to resistance to the new leader's efforts.

5. **LEADERS DEMONSTRATE EXCELLENT COMMUNICATION SKILLS:** As previously illustrated, Quick Wins require communication. Leaders must be good communicators from conveying the vision and strategy to using communication skills for coaching and feedback. With solid communication skills, leaders can succeed.

6. **LEADERS DEMONSTRATE ENABLING SKILLS:** This characteristic is about empowerment. The turnaround process will be accelerated by empowering people to make decisions, work together, and focus on critical needs. Leaders can demonstrate enabling skills by setting expectations for

decision-making, drawing clear lines of when and where the team can make decisions, and fundamentally providing the time and resources needed to enable performance to happen.

7. **LEADERS REINFORCE TEAM-BUILDING SKILLS:** We must recognize the power of the team during the turnaround process. This characteristic should be first on the list during a turnaround, which requires "all hands on deck" as a team to engage in working together to drive change. Leaders who reinforce team-building skills will accelerate the turnaround process.

8. **LEADERS CONFRONT ADVERSITY:** Leaders do not avoid adversity; they confront it head-on. Taking the time to understand why adversity exists, what's at the root, and collaborating toward a solution can be the differentiator between success and failure. During the turnaround process, leaders will face challenging goals, problems with people implementing the change, and even the magnitude of the change itself. In the end, leaders must be proactive, not reactive, to manage the change with minimal adversity.

9. **LEADERS DEVELOP A CULTURE:** If you remember, culture is "How we do things around here." Culture can be decades old or newly minted. From how administrators roam the school hallways to break times for educators and staff, "How we do things around here" can take many forms. For leaders during a turnaround process, developing the right culture requires leadership to understand and define "How we *want* to do things around here."

Quick Wins are critical to moving toward such a culture, but without a clear goal of what the culture looks like, the question is, "What kind of culture are we going to end up with?" By focusing on developing a culture, leaders can achieve great performance, long-lasting change, and a turnaround that stands the test of time.

From these nine characteristics, leaders can narrow their focus during the turnaround to achieve various Quick Wins.

Leadership Requirements for Initiating and Sustaining Quick Wins

There are many different types of leaders and if you listen to more than one leader, you are likely to notice several differences in their "style" of leadership. In short, their behavioral tendencies. But even though their styles differ, if you lift the hood, you will find that the most successful leaders build their leadership on common ground. They adhere to common principles and approaches, many of which are found in this book. Regarding leadership approaches required to initiate and sustain Quick Wins, the following three requirements are fundamental to success regardless of a leader's "style":

1. Quick Wins require leaders to *seek feedback*

2. Quick Wins require leaders to *be a positive stimulus*

3.   Quick Wins require leaders to *implement systematic feedback using a tiered approach:*

   • Tier I— Learning new skills requires practice

   • Tier II—Feedback should be equitable, not equal

   • Tier III—Performance management is necessary for ongoing success

We'll discuss each of these requirements in the following pages.

1. Quick Wins—Require leaders to seek feedback

During a turnaround, leaders are busy, nervous, and even fearful at times, given the often-intense needs of the school. To achieve success in a turnaround environment, leaders must engage their team to achieve Quick Wins. They engage others by demonstrating leadership that people will follow. Because there's so much at stake, leaders often wonder if they are doing the right things.

Well, don't wonder: Ask! By soliciting feedback from your team, you can get a clear pulse on your performance as a leader. Organizations worldwide employ various leadership-feedback methods, such as feedback surveys, interviews, focus groups, and upward feedback reports. Such feedback is so common in business today that, in some unideal cases, leaders receive more feedback than do employees. Even with this positive trend for business leaders to seek feedback, leadership feedback has only recently gained some ground in education.

By seeking feedback on your leadership behaviors during a turnaround, you are getting what could be the most critical data to achieve success—namely, information that allows you to determine how much you are helping or hurting the situation.

Essentially, feedback on leadership behaviors provides an opportunity for the people around you—your employees, your peers, your supervisors—to let you know how they think you are performing as a leader. What you are looking for are patterns of common feedback from multiple sources. For example,

   • How do you set expectations—are you confused or clear?

   • What does your presence do to people—do they run or smile?

   • How is your feedback received—is it harsh or helpful?

This feedback on your leadership behavior will give you deep insight into how those around you perceive your leadership behaviors and, more importantly, the impact you have on their performance, the school environment, and the probability of turnaround success. These data allow you to change your behavior to support your people, support the school's performance, or make the turnaround much more successful.

Principal Daniels initially solicited feedback weekly from his faculty and staff using a brief and anonymous survey during Monday morning "huddles." During these debriefs, the principal met with faculty and staff to discuss the previous week's progress toward goals, make any needed adjustments, and set goals for the next week. During this time, he issued the paper-and-pencil survey and asked them to rate five statements on a scale from 1–5:

1. I feel safe.

2. I believe we are moving in a positive direction.

3. My leader has my best interests in mind.

4. I feel supported by the leadership team.

5. I feel as though I have input in the direction of the school.

The survey also included two open-ended responses; "I like ..." and "I wish we could change ... ." Each Monday, at the end of the day, Principal Daniels met with his leadership team to review the survey data, graph trends, and address any pattern of concerns.

We will dive back into other sources of feedback in a later chapter as we discuss 360-degree feedback surveys and leadership development.

2. Quick Wins—Require leaders to be a positive stimulus

We can remember one time giving a presentation to a large group of teachers in the school's media center the year before our principal came to the school to turn it around. The teachers were highly engaged. They were asking questions, making comments, smiling, and occasionally laughing! But suddenly, things got very quiet. The questions stopped. No more comments. And you would think we were at a funeral, as no smiles were seen across the room. Laughter came to a screeching halt, like after a bad joke in a comedy club.

What happened? It did not take long to determine the cause: The principal had entered through the side door. He walked in, scanned the room, looked at the presenter, and gave a nod to gesture, "Hello." He then sat in the chair nearest the door, suggesting that he might leave shortly, as he intermittently looked at his phone. His very presence changed everything. In short, this school principal was not a positive stimulus.

How will you know if you are a positive stimulus during a turnaround? Well, you might be thinking that survey data can best inform you. And it might. But there are also times that—even when the school leader does their best to ensure anonymity—faculty, and staff may still be afraid to respond honestly. Perhaps it's that they were punished for it in the past. Or, perhaps, you have yet to establish yourself as a positive stimulus.

Ask yourself these questions:

• How do my staff behave in my presence?

- How do my staff behave in my absence?

- What have I said or done when I've observed them performing well?

- What have I said or done when I've observed them performing poorly?

Your answers will help you discover whether you are a positive or negative stimulus for your staff. Much as we observe a classroom and discern very quickly what behaviors have been targeted and reinforced by the teacher, we can observe the behaviors of the staff in the leader's presence and absence to determine what key behaviors have been reinforced quickly. As a leader, your behavior, or inaction, will tremendously impact your staff's performance. We mention inaction because sometimes doing nothing to behavior is like doing something. More on that in a minute.

During a turnaround, it is critical for leaders to be a positive stimulus for desired staff behavior. Think of yourself as the traffic light and your staff's behavior as the vehicle. What does your presence signal your staff to do? Does it tell them to interact positively with students, stand in a particular area in the cafeteria, or use a targeted instructional strategy they were recently trained on? How staff behaves in your presence directly indicates the values you've modeled and the behaviors you've reinforced or corrected.

By setting performance goals and providing performance feedback as a norm, staff will be cued or "reminded" of these goals in your presence. When this happens, staff will at least attempt the targeted behavior, which allows you to reinforce small changes, correct, or help them see the meaningful consequences of their behavior (e.g., increased engagement, decreased misbehavior, or improved achievement scores).

When you target small goals and provide consistent, deliberate feedback to staff, *your presence* will evoke your desired performance. You do not have to say a word, and your staff's behavior will change. *"Sometimes doing nothing is doing something to performance"* (Daniels, 2016, p. 29)!

What if no meaningful consequence occurred due to braking at the traffic light? Let's suspend disbelief for a moment as we do at the movies. What if the traffic light appears in the middle of nowhere, with no other cars in sight, no cop present, and you are in a rush? Would you stop? Some of us would because of the guilt that might occur after years of operating under normal traffic rules. However, many of us would likely roll through the light, no harm done!

Sticking with the driving scenario, what if law enforcement *never* gave speeding tickets? Would you continue to double-check your speed or slow in their presence?

Or, let's reverse the strategy. What if, instead of giving drivers tickets for speeding, law enforcement intermittently pulled over law-abiding drivers and gave them a $100 discount on their insurance? How might that impact your behavior?

The point is simply the presence of a traffic light, or an officer can *cue* certain behaviors when there are known consequences (ticket or reward). But when no consequences are in place (no ticket, no reward), what do you think would happen? There are just too many possibilities!

People tend to behave in ways that suit *them* best, which may not necessarily align with the law, school rules, or your turnaround goals.

Let's take an educational example of a teacher attempting a new skill. They will be far more likely to keep working on it if the effort is recognized by the leader. On the other hand, they'll be far less likely to continue trying it if they aren't experiencing a positive impact and the leader does not recognize the effort. In contrast, the teacher who repeatedly reprimands students in the leader's presence will likely continue to do so without feedback from the leader. In a sense, failing to correct the teacher's behavior is the same as condoning it. Be aware of how the staff behaves in your presence. As much as possible, positively reinforce what is aligned with the school's stated vision, mission, and values, and correct what is not.

3. Quick Wins—Require leaders to implement systematic feedback using a tiered approach

By focusing your leadership role on becoming a positive stimulus, you can trigger the behavior you need for a successful turnaround.

We recognize the importance of effective feedback for enabling Quick Wins and for supporting the overall success of school improvement efforts. In a perfect world, all faculty and staff would need the same amount of feedback to achieve the desired performance state. But in the real world, school leaders should treat their staff *equitably* (as opposed to equally) to reach the desired goals.

Just as it's important to provide differentiated instruction to students to meet their needs, staff require differentiated approaches to feedback to support their needs. There is an approach called *situational leadership* that nicely supports the need for equitability. It recommends a continuum of the directive and supportive behavior based on the follower's needs (Hersey et al., 2001).

But determining the needs of your staff and differentiating your approach can be a challenge, to say the least. For this reason, we recommend using Response to Intervention (RTI) logic to systematically support staff based on their need when implementing school-wide initiatives.

RTI, a common approach used across many states, is a multitiered (Tier I, II, & III) approach that attempts to support academic and behavioral success through universal screening, quick intervention, frequent measurement, and progressively intensive instruction or interventions for students who continue to have difficulty. This approach can be easily applied when seeking to achieve Quick Wins.

- Tier I provides universal training to all staff (e.g., teachers), with simple follow-up feedback to shape behavior.

- Tier II provides retraining and brief follow-up coaching to a targeted group of educators who do not perform to the established criteria during the initial Tier I training.

- Tier III, much like situational leadership, focuses on the specific needs of the individual (e.g., managing response rates, using standards and scales, etc.). These staff would receive focused coaching to meet the individual needs of educators who did not respond (perform to standard) to the Tier II intervention.

Let's take a deeper look at the multitiered approach, using a familiar concept for getting the most out of your feedback during and following a turnaround.

Tier I—Learning New Skills Requires Practice

Unfortunately, too many teachers and staff are provided "sit and gets" as professional development, and then they are expected to perform a newly learned skill to some established standard. For many years researchers have found there is often far too much theory and far too little practice during professional development endeavors (Joyce & Showers, 2002). If "sit and gets" worked, we wouldn't be writing this book!

The good news is that, during initial professional development, there are three simple strategies to promote the generalization of newly learned and developing skills as part of a Tier I approach. This is important when you are establishing Quick Wins, as well as for fostering sustainable change.

FIRST: LESS TALK, MORE PRACTICE—During training to build fluency, leaders must ensure frequent repetition and performance feedback for targeted skills. In other words: less talk, more practice. To engage the teacher in the learning process toward achieving fluency, Parsons et al. (2013) recommend that skills training occurs in this sequence:

1. Require the performer to describe the target skill

2. Provide performers with a precise written description of the target skill

3. Demonstrate the target skill for the performer

4. Require the performer to deliberately practice the skill

5. Give performer-specific feedback during practice

6. Repeat steps 4 and 5 (practice and feedback) until the target skill is mastered

This sequence fosters a *significant gain* of knowledge and skill. When educators understand the expectations and can perform the skill, the feedback leaders provide during the normal school day is *much* more likely to improve the skill's effectiveness significantly. While on-the-job feedback is often required to generalize newly learned skills, this training process frequently eliminates the need for more time- and resource-consuming strategies such as in-depth coaching and further training.

With a brief shot of **QUICK** feedback from the leadership team that will be discussed shortly, staff will be much more likely to observe meaningful change due to their newly acquired skill. Changes such as increased student engagement, improved behavior, and gains in academic achievement will strengthen self-efficacy while strengthening belief in you as a leader.

SECOND: USE WALKABOUTS—We will learn more about walkabouts in a later chapter. The purpose of walkabouts is to increase visibility and provide positive feedback during the initial phases of any new school-wide initiative. This allows the leadership to strengthen relationships while keeping things moving in the right direction. What leaders do and say daily as they walk the hallways is far more critical than what is said in a meeting. Leaders are constantly evaluated, so this is when leaders can establish themselves as a positive stimulus by conveying warmth and knowledge in a way that helps staff feel safe and cared for.

This heightened visibility and positive interactions and feedback effectively build momentum. Any feedback that results in meaningful and positive consequences for staff strengthens the belief that the leader respects them, is knowledgeable, and can be trusted.

THIRD: BE AWARE OF YOUR NONVERBAL BEHAVIORS DURING WALKABOUTS. According to Goman (2011) in *The Silent Language of Leaders*, presidential elections are lost or won not by where the candidate stands on issues but rather *by the warmth and confidence conveyed during the election*. Behaviorally this means that leaders should use "open body postures, palm-up hand gestures, a full-frontal body orientation, positive eye contact, synchronized movements, head nods, head tilts, and smiles" (Goman, 2011, p. 25). By deliberately walking around, leaders are physically present to ask how the staff is doing, how the new initiative is going, and to focus on *catching staff performing well*. The leadership team can quickly accelerate any new initiative with walkabouts. Because using feedback as a tiered strategy supports any new initiative, leaders will build relationships with their teams and support them at every step of the learning and change process.

This is Tier I—train to fluency to accelerate change. Incorporating the above strategies into any initial training you hold will help quickly generalize the training objectives into the classroom.

The QUICK Feedback Approach

To increase the efficiency and effectiveness of feedback while demonstrating your care, use **QUICK** feedback as a Tier I process during walkabouts:

Questions: Ask them!

Unconditional positive regard (Rogers, 1956): Provide it.

Immediate positive reinforcement of any observed improvement in performance: Provide it.

Constructive feedback: Deliver it to coach staff through minor errors or when staff solicits it.

Keep feedback brief, and meaningful: Frequency and brevity are key to this approach.

Here's a closer look—

QUESTIONS—At the root of questioning during the QUICK feedback process is demonstrating that the leader is invested in the well-being of staff and the change. Questions can be simple, such as *How is your day? How are you doing with the new changes? Do you need help?*

UNCONDITIONAL POSITIVE REGARD—Known as "noncontingent attention" in the behavioral sciences, unconditional positive regard captures the essence of strengthening relationships with team members while establishing the leader as a reinforcer.

IMMEDIATE POSITIVE REINFORCEMENT—Provides high value to those who demonstrate improved performance and further builds the relationship between the leader and staff.

CONSTRUCTIVE FEEDBACK—Allows leadership to correct and then later reinforce performance in a way that helps staff grow. The intent here is to help, not hinder.

KEEP FEEDBACK BRIEF—Your attention is powerful and in demand. While you want to be available, your time is limited, so by deliberately keeping it brief, you can increase positive interactions with more team members.

Tier II—Feedback Should Be Equitable, Not Equal

Even with excellent training using the approaches above, typically, approximately 15% to 20% of your faculty and staff need further support (Ennis et al., 2020). Educators who do not respond effectively to your universal Tier I approach, as observed during walkabouts, should receive additional support as a Tier II QUICK intervention.

Instead of thinning your resources with individual coaching, Tier II efficiently supports educators through a brief group retrain, followed by frequent but brief follow-up observations with feedback on targeted skills. This group retrains using the training sequence listed above. Still, because much fewer staff are involved, they gain the opportunity to receive increased repetition and feedback to build greater fluency in targeted skills. Moreover, you can focus walkabouts and brief coaching interactions on this group to assist with generalizing their skills into the school or classroom.

Tier III—Performance Management for Ongoing Success

If the Tier II approach goes as intended, you should be left with approximately 1%–5% of the faculty and staff who may still be struggling (Ennis et al., 2020). Tier III approaches the managing of staff performance like a coach, using ongoing performance monitoring and feedback. For you, this is not about taking an individual approach to performance but rather a systematic approach to managing the team's performance. This involves you or designees (e.g., assistant principals, coaches) giving faculty and staff opportunities to demonstrate their skills, provide feedback, and set/reinforce goals to shape targeted skills.

You should see Tier III as your ongoing feedback process versus the first two tiers, which have an expiration date following training. When instructional coaches are available, you can direct them to staff who need Tier III interventions.

Strategic Planning With the End in Mind

We've just unpacked the three leadership requirements to get Quick Wins going:

1. Quick Wins require each leader to *seek feedback*

2. Quick Wins require each leader to *be a positive stimulus*

3. Quick Wins require each leader to *implement systematic feedback using a tiered approach*

Launching Quick Wins are going to be one thing, but if you truly want to keep them going, you need to have a good system in place. A good system starts with the end in mind and leverages all of the important leadership strategies we've just highlighted. To maximize the impact of Quick Wins, school leaders are best served by starting with the end in mind. In other words, what is the result you are trying to produce with your Quick Win? Is it improved student achievement? Improved discipline? Improved morale? Whatever it is, stop focusing on the individual or even group performance of faculty and staff, and refocus some of your energies on looking at the system. *(See Figure 3.1 on the following page.)*

For example, one of the Quick Wins Principal Daniels and the stakeholders wanted to focus on as a goal was improving student behavior during arrival. To do this, he guided his team by starting with the desired result. Starting with the end in mind is a common approach to instructional design and lesson planning. In other words, what is the desired learning outcome?

This same concept applies to engineering Quick Wins. Start with the desired outcome or result. In this case, reducing the number of high-magnitude behavior challenges occurring during arrival was measured by the number of office discipline referrals submitted. To reduce office discipline referrals, the team had to determine:

- What student behavior will achieve the intended results?

- What teacher behaviors are likely to create the student outcomes?

- What teachers and staff need from educator support personnel?

- What educator support is needed from their leadership to help them demonstrate the necessary behavior?

- What, if anything, does leadership need from the district that will promote the desired teacher and student behavior?

Strategic Planning With the End in Mind Schoolwide

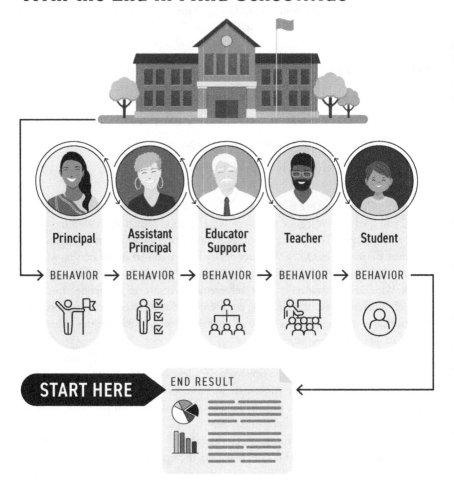

FIGURE 3.1: *Improving outcomes by starting with the end result and then aligning behavior with it.*

The collective behaviors that make up a series of tasks and processes ultimately define the system for achieving the Quick Win. Employing this logic, Principal Daniels and his team of stakeholders decided that student discipline would be addressed through a systems approach that linked students' behavior with teachers' behavior, teachers' behavior with the leadership team's behavior, and the leadership teams' behavior with the principal's behavior. For example:

- **End Result:** reduced high-magnitude behavior

- **Measure:** office discipline referrals (ODRs)

- **Student Behavior:** following arrival expectations

- **Faculty & Staff Behavior:**

   ° During class, providing the "why" for following expectations during arrival

   ° Greeting students as they arrive

   ° Interacting positively and using behavior-specific praise as they follow expectations four times as much as they correct behavior (4:1 ratio)

   ° Immediately correcting behavior by having the students state and demonstrate the expectations

- **Administrator Behavior:**

   ° Explaining the why behind the Quick Win

   ° Seeking feedback and input from faculty, staff, and students

   ° Using the input to agree on expectations

   ° Creating a map of faculty and staff arrival duty posts

   ° Providing a brief in-service to allow faculty and staff to rehearse the expectations

   ° Observing and positively reinforcing faculty and staff for being at their posts and adhering to expectations at a 4:1 ratio

   ° Correcting errors in faculty and staff performance

   ° Sharing the ODR data daily via email during the initial launch

   ° Providing positive reinforcement with statements that align their behavior with the positive outcomes (e.g., "Because you all are at your posts greeting students, positively reinforcing and correcting student behavior, we've already had a 15% reduction in ODRs. Great job!")

   ° Fading as the data suggest. For example, after a week's worth of success, emails are fading to every other day, then weekly, and finally to monthly reports.

By starting with the end in mind and identifying these behaviors, Principal Daniels and his team outlined a clear behavioral path of what educators would need to do more, less, or differently to achieve the intended result. This plan provided clear direction to everybody while allowing the leadership team to teach, observe, positively reinforce, and correct performance errors up the chain. This also put Principal Daniels and his team in a position to deliberately and systematically provide feedback that aligned individual and collective behavior with results. You see, achieving quicks wins is all about behavior, results, and leadership, establishing a clear system that provides multiple opportunities to positively reinforce everybody's behavior up the chain—that is, the behavior of students, staff, faculty, and even members of the leadership team.

Once critical behaviors are identified and aligned at each level within the school, the school leader or team should engage in practical performance diagnostics when a teacher or leader is not performing to a standard. Have you ever wondered why people don't do what they should do? Performance diagnostics allow for precise intervention as it helps you discover why someone is not performing to a standard and helps you determine the root cause of performance issues to target support. Typically, people aren't performing well for two simple reasons: They "can't do" or "won't do." The individual lacks the skill to perform the task or behavior, or lacks motivation. Most people immediately think that training is the answer to solving performance issues. But not everybody needs training, and training is an expensive resource in terms of cost, time, and human resources. Some individuals just need reminders, more efficient processes, or maybe just a little coaching to get them in touch with valued outcomes by engaging in the right behavior. In the next chapter, we will dive deeper into how to identify and address performance issues using a tool called the Performance Diagnostic Checklist.

The glue that holds an effective system together is positive reinforcement. This means that school leaders, the leadership team, and classroom leaders (teachers) should be trained to shape performance. Shaping performance is the process of reinforcing successive approximations toward the desired goal. As part of this process, remember that leaders should emphasize using positive reinforcement through effective feedback. Leaders who understand and effectively use QUICK feedback to positively reinforce behavior are much more likely to create learning environments. Because the shaping process utilizes positive reinforcement from a strength-based perspective, it typically improves the climate and culture of schools as faculty and staff are primarily recognized for what they are doing right and then provided feedback on how they can become even better. And the students are treated in the same fashion.

The final practical approach would be to measure leaders based on the improvement of those they directly supervise. The measure of a teacher would be found in students' performance; the measure of the leadership team in teachers' performance. In turn, the measure of the principal would be found in the performance of their leadership team and, therefore, in the performance of all. In the end, the success or failure of a school turnaround can be directly tied back to leadership.

For schools to change, systems must align and operate effectively with each other, beginning from the top (Hall & Hord, 2011). This means if you are a leader, you must strategically plan with the end in mind to launch and sustain your Quick Wins. This will allow you to increase learning and improve instruction through a collective, aligned, and systematic approach aimed at an important end result that you are attempting to achieve.

Quick Takeaways:

- The leadership requirements for initiating and sustaining Quick Wins require the leaders to seek feedback, be a positive stimulus, and implement a system for providing feedback using a three-tiered approach.

- Performance diagnostics help determine why people don't perform well.

- There are two reasons for performance issues: "can't do" or "won't do." The individual lacks the skill or motivation to complete the task or engage in the behavior.

- Leaders who understand and effectively use QUICK feedback to positively reinforce are much more likely to create learning environments.

- Quick Wins will only sustain with an effective system in place.

- Starting with the result or outcome will help school leaders maximize the impact of Quick Wins. Identify the result you are trying to produce with your Quick Win.

- For schools to change, systems must align and operate effectively with each other through strategic planning with the end in mind.

Sustain It:

- What are some examples of behaviors for each of these nine leadership characteristics integral to turning around a school?

   1. Leaders provide a value proposition

   2. Leaders show ethical values

   3. Leaders demonstrate execution skills

   4. Leaders encourage innovation and creativity

   5. Leaders demonstrate excellent communication skills

   6. Leaders demonstrate enabling skills

   7. Leaders reinforce team-building skills

   8. Leaders confront adversity

   9. Leaders develop a culture

- In what ways could you solicit input from faculty and staff?

- ° What are some indicators that they are willing to share this information with you?

- ° As a leader, what would you do to ensure that you were accountable for the feedback provided?

- It is essential for any school environment that leaders establish themselves as a positive stimulus.

- ° What might be some of those behaviors?

- ° Describe them

- How would you know you are a positive stimulus in your school? What behaviors would you observe from the faculty and staff?

CHAPTER 4:

Quick Wins Require QuickWOCs

Recognizing Quick Wins: The Quick Win Matrix

Now that we've unpacked leadership and systematic approaches to initiating and sustaining Quick Wins, let's take a look at identifying them. Leaders will be able to recognize a Quick Win by using the *Quick Win Matrix* to evaluate any opportunity based on the combination of impact, visibility, and effort. The Quick Win Matrix (Figure 4.1) gives you a visual tool for prioritizing Quick Wins. The graphic illustrates the linkage between impact, visibility, and effort:

- The higher the impact and the lower the effort, the better the Quick Win.

- It's not good enough to hold high-impact value—the Quick Win must be visible.

- If the Quick Win is high-impact and high-visibility, but the effort is too high, requiring lots of resources and possibly external support, the Quick Win may not be practical to pursue.

The school leader can achieve Quick Wins for the turnaround by focusing on impact, visibility, and effort.

Leaders working with school staff can evaluate the impact, visibility, and effort using a simple high-medium-low scale. As you can see, the ideal Quick Win has high impact, high visibility, and low effort.

Impact, Visibility, and Effort

Leaders of school turnarounds can stand confident in their decisions on which Quick Wins to implement. Here's how it works:

1. Make a complete list of all the tasks needed to produce change at the school and place them under the "Potential Quick Wins List."

2. Sort the potential Quick Win based on the impact, visibility, and effort.

3. Give Quick Wins the highest priority and start with those tasks.

4. After the Quick Win, address potential "Low-Hanging Fruit" and "Future Projects."

5. Place those projects that are high effort and low impact under "Resource Drainers." Consider how you might minimize the effort and increase the impact of these tasks to transform them into Quick Wins.

Quick Win Matrix

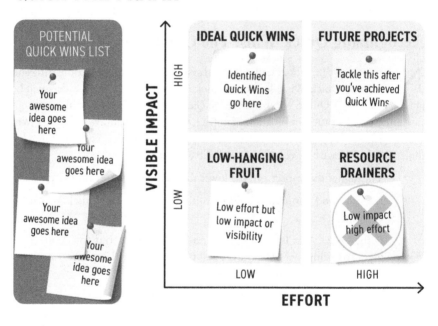

FIGURE 4.1: The Quick Win Matrix is a tool that can determine which Quick Win to implement out of an array of potential tasks needed to produce change at the school. The matrix is divided into four categories and includes an area to list potential Quick Wins. The identified Quick Win goes in the "Ideal Quick Wins" box. This task is selected because it meets high impact, visibility, and low effort criteria. Those tasks listed under "Low-Hanging Fruit" are considered tasks requiring low effort but having low impact or visibility. The projects to tackle after achieving the ideal Quick Win are listed under the "Future Projects" category. And "Resource Drainers" are those projects or tasks considered low impact with high effort.

Principal Daniels and his leadership team faced another set of issues that could be immediately addressed through potential Quick Wins after the first month of school: improving the traffic pattern in the parking lot and improving communications between administrators, faculty, and staff regarding disruptive behavior. He remembered being stuck in the school's car loop traffic the year before, and nothing had changed there as the original Quick Wins had been receiving all the focus. Faculty, staff, parents, and the community were unhappy about the traffic challenges that were arising. It was causing many people to be late. He also recognized a problematic pattern developing regarding discipline and communication in the form of students being sent out of the classroom for behavior challenges. There was no process for communicating and problem-solving regarding the data because there was not even a process for collecting it. Students were just being sent out! These challenges required attention to keep the behavioral momentum moving in the right direction.

FIGURE 4.2: *The ideal Quick Win is in the upper left box because it meets all the criteria of high impact, high visibility, and low effort. Each Quick Win identified is categorized using the matrix to determine the most significant Quick Wins.*

Quick Win Matrix

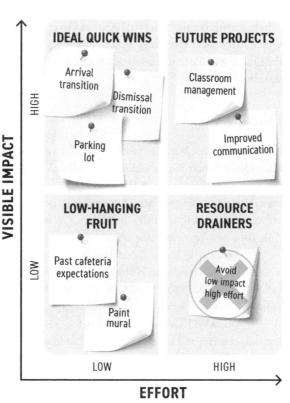

Principal Daniels and his leadership team used the Quick Win Matrix to address these issues. Both potential Quick Wins were considered high value. Specifically, the "parking lot" increased the impact of safety and efficiency, and "improving communications" increased the value of communicating using data to mitigate problem behavior.

IMPACT: Both Quick Wins were considered high value.

VISIBILITY: Improving the parking lot traffic pattern would be seen by all who came to the school—specifically, during drop-off and pickup times—so this Quick Win would be high in visibility. However, the second Quick Win of improving communications was visible only to those who would be part of the communication (i.e., the principal, vice principal, security, and the teacher reporting the problem behavior), so this Quick Win would be low in visibility.

EFFORT: The venture to achieve each Quick Win was different. The resources to improve communications (i.e., new technology, training, and a clear data collection and review procedure) would take up to a month to complete, while the school parking lot traffic pattern changes could be made in a day. Thus, the school traffic pattern required less effort than the much higher effort required for improving communication.

Though each was valued, the parking lot was prioritized as the first Quick Win to pursue because it scored higher in low effort and high visibility. Though both Quick Wins were eventually accomplished, by prioritizing change initiatives with the Quick Win Matrix, school leaders could demonstrate real, immediate value to all stakeholders quickly.

QuickWOC

Identifying Quick Wins can (and should!) be a *quick* process. The first step to identifying Quick Wins requires walking around, making direct observations, and conversing with people throughout the school. (This seems obvious, but sometimes folks miss the obvious, so it is essential to state it.) The best school improvement efforts are reflected by this simple truth—*if I don't see it, hear it, or understand what's going on from those who live it, how can I effectively change it?*

Those who know about daily happenings are the most critical in this step. To help you facilitate your *observations* and *conversations*, we have developed a tool called *QuickWOC*. Pronounced "quick walk," the acronym stands for: **W** = Walking around, **O** = Observations, **C** = Conversations.

QuickWOC allows the leader to focus on specific areas and behaviors to walk around, observe, and converse when determining where a Quick Win could make a positive difference for students and teachers (The Doing What Works Library, n.d.).

QuickWOC identifies other sources of information to help identify opportunities for improvement that may be addressed beyond the short term.

Using a QuickWOC

A QuickWOC has three parts:

- Part 1—Walkabout Observations
- Part 2—Other Sources
- Part 3—Performance Diagnostic Checklist

PART 1—WALKABOUT OBSERVATIONS. The walkabout is a walking tour of school facilities. This can be done in a group that includes administrators, teachers, and students. If necessary, it can be done individually. Walk through the building at different times during the school day, on different days, before and after school. Observe the elements listed in QuickWOC that might be corrected with immediate, focused, simple reforms. Note where you see problems occurring.

When planning to engage in the QuickWOC process, the QuickWOC form lists recommended areas for the team to observe. The tool also lists questions to guide your thinking. The questions on the QuickWOC form address various common areas of the school, such as arrival and dismissal zones, the cafeteria, and classrooms. In addition, you may identify other places in the school to observe (e.g., portables, trailers, gymnasiums, auditoriums, etc.). These highly visible areas often are problematic in turnaround schools and can bring a Quick Win.

Use this scoring rubric:

QuickWOC Part 1—Walkabout Observations

The QuickWOC is a collaborative approach for identifying Quick Wins for school turnaround efforts. The QuickWOC observation form is divided into seven domains that ask questions about the most visible common areas of the school. The areas identified are typically problematic during a school turnaround. For each question in the domain during the walkabout observation, rate it using the Likert scale.

Domain	Score				
ARRIVAL/DISMISSAL	1 Never	2 Rarely	3 Sometimes	4 Often	5 Always
1. Students walk during transitions.					
2. Students follow communication expectations (e.g., they speak at a conversational level).					
3. Students follow a designated route.					

Domain	Score				
ARRIVAL/DISMISSAL	1 Never	2 Rarely	3 Sometimes	4 Often	5 Always
4. Students transition directly to the designated area per the school's expectations.					
5. Staff attend their post on time.					
6. Staff stand in assigned areas.					
7. Staff greet the students and positively interact with them.					
8. Staff consistently correct misbehavior.					
9. When correcting misbehavior, staff use a calm and respectful manner.					
10. When a student runs, staff require the student to walk back to where they began running.					
11. Students transition safely to their transportation.					
12. Students move on and off the sidewalk in an orderly manner.					
13. Students have safe, designated areas to sit or stand while waiting for transportation.					
14. The front office staff smile at parents, students, and visitors when they enter the front office.					
15. The front office staff greet parents, students, and visitors (e.g., "Good morning," "We'll be right with you.").					
16. When answering the phone, the front office staff communicate in ways that convey respect, kindness, and an "at your service" attitude.					

Domain	Score				
HALLWAYS	1 Never	2 Rarely	3 Sometimes	4 Often	5 Always

1. Students walk during transitions.

2. Students follow communication expectations (e.g., they speak at a conversational level).

3. Students follow a designated route.

4. Students transition directly to the designated area per the school's expectations.

5. Staff attend their post on time.

6. Staff stand in assigned areas.

7. Staff constantly monitor their assigned area.

8. Staff greet the students or provide random positive attention.

9. Staff consistently correct misbehavior.

10. When correcting misbehavior, staff use a calm and respectful manner.

11. When a student runs, staff require the student to walk back to where they began running.

Domain	Score				
CAFETERIA	1 Never	2 Rarely	3 Sometimes	4 Often	5 Always

1. Students transition through the line efficiently.

2. It is easy for students to find seating (finding a seat creates little to no tension among students).

3. Students pick up trash and deposit it in the correct containers.

Domain	Score				
CAFETERIA	1 Never	2 Rarely	3 Sometimes	4 Often	5 Always
4. Students follow expectations when they have finished eating.					
5. Students face forward with their feet on the ground.					
6. Students talk only to the students at their table and do not yell across tables.					
7. Students ask permission or follow school expectations before leaving their seats or area.					
8. Staff stand at assigned posts.					
9. Staff actively scan their assigned areas.					
10. Staff track potential problems and intervene early.					
11. Staff greet the students and positively interact with them.					
12. Staff consistently correct misbehaviors such as students leaving their area without permission or yelling across tables.					
13. Staff provide more positive interactions than corrections.					
14. Staff follow through on warnings for repeated misbehavior.					
15. Staff refrain from grouping and speaking amongst themselves.					

Domain	Score				
PLAYGROUNDS/FIELDS	1 Never	2 Rarely	3 Sometimes	4 Often	5 Always
1. There are identified boundaries.					
2. The equipment is organized and easy to access.					

Domain	Score				
PLAYGROUNDS/FIELDS	1 Never	2 Rarely	3 Sometimes	4 Often	5 Always
3. Students use the playground equipment safely.					
4. The equipment is clean and safe.					
5. Staff consistently monitor students.					
6. Staff refrain from grouping and speaking among themselves.					
7. Staff actively scan their assigned areas.					
8. Staff track potential problems and intervene early.					

Domain	Score				
BATHROOMS	1 Never	2 Rarely	3 Sometimes	4 Often	5 Always
1. There are identified boundaries.					
2. Students enter the bathrooms in reasonable numbers (i.e., only a few students in the bathroom at one time).					
3. Students use the facility for its intended purpose.					
4. Bathroom areas have procedures that ensure students will not congregate.					
5. Staff monitor the bathroom areas to check for safety and cleanliness.					

Domain	Score				
CLASSROOMS	1 Never	2 Rarely	3 Sometimes	4 Often	5 Always
1. Students respond in a well-behaved manner toward the teacher and other adults in the room.					

Domain	Score				
CLASSROOMS	1 Never	2 Rarely	3 Sometimes	4 Often	5 Always
2. Students respect the materials and property in the classroom.					
3. Students respect their fellow students.					
4. Core subject areas receive uninterrupted blocks of time.					
5. Classrooms have established routines and procedures that include behavioral expectations for all activities and transitions.					

Domain	Score				
FACILITIES	1 Never	2 Rarely	3 Sometimes	4 Often	5 Always
1. The school façade or school grounds appear to be in good condition.					
2. The inside of the building, including bathrooms, hallways, storage areas, and teacher workrooms, are in good condition.					
3. Classrooms have enough storage cabinets, space, etc., to maintain a clean and orderly environment for learning.					
4. Students and teachers access materials easily and quickly.					

PART 2—OTHER SOURCES. Helps you seek input from other sources of information, such as reports from professionals who deliver services in the schools, for identifying potential Quick Wins.

The principal and leadership team may wish to collect information through meetings, informal conversations, and focus-group discussions with other school staff, parents, and possibly students. The principal and leadership team can also analyze data (discipline data, climate data, etc.) to identify areas of potential Quick Wins. The QuickWOC is also a great tool to use before starting a new school year. During this time, the leader can seek qualitative data from people in the know, including parents, teachers, and district employees.

QuickWOC Part 2—Other Sources

Additional Sources of Information	Observation Notes
STAFF	
1. What changes could be made easily and quickly that would make a difference to staff doing their daily work?	
2. Are there materials and resources that staff need?	
PARENTS	
3. What areas do parents think need to change quickly to improve the school environment and help their children learn?	
COMMUNITY	
4. Are there changes that could occur quickly and make a difference to the community and its perception of the school?	
OBSERVATION TEAM	
5. What are the most pervasive problems identified by the team?	
6. How do the team's observations align with comments from staff, parents, and the community?	
OF THESE PROBLEMS, WHICH ONES COULD BE MOST EASILY REMEDIED?	

PART 3—PERFORMANCE DIAGNOSTIC CHECKLIST. Once the Quick Wins were identified, Principal Daniels and his team needed a better understanding of the root cause of the issues to be addressed. During the meeting, one of the leadership team members blurted out, "Why won't they do it? How do I get staff to do what I need them to do, meaning, how EXACTLY do you do it?"

"Tell me more," Principal Daniels encouraged.

The team member went on to explain that both the previous year and this year, she had told her staff what to do in terms of collecting discipline data and reporting discipline issues. She even showed them how to do it. When that didn't work, she tried rewarding the staff with donuts on Tuesdays or fun activity on Fridays. Still, not everyone complied. Next, she explained, she reprimanded the staff by sending "punishing" emails listing all the punishment that would occur if they didn't collect data.

After all of that, she shared that only a couple of faculty began to collect data. "I have tried EVERYTHING!" she said. After listening to her story, Principal Daniels asked *why* she thought the faculty and staff were not doing what she asked them to do. "They just don't care. I trained them, and they don't care. I support multiple classrooms and have lots of other responsibilities. I just ended up collecting the data myself. It was just too much; trying to get them to do what I needed them to do."

So, Principal Daniels asked a few more questions:

Daniels: "Did you give your staff a written description of exactly how to collect data?"

Team Member: "Well, no, I showed them."

Daniels: "OK, what about formal training on data collection?"

Team Member: "Well, they had all been at the school before and were supposed to collect data. I assumed they knew how to collect data."

Daniels: "Did the faculty and staff know the expectation and the 'WHY' or importance of data collection?"

Team Member: "They knew it was part of their job, and they were expected to collect data daily."

Daniels: "OK, were they given a data collection protocol?"

Team Member: "Well, no."

Daniels: "What about data sheets and colored pencils and highlighters, graph paper? Were they given data collection tools?"

Team Member: "I made lots of copies of data sheets."

Principal Daniels and the leadership team member continued their conversation and could have spent most of the meeting on this topic. In his final questions, Principal Daniels asked the team member to think about staff performance and how often she or another leadership team member monitored the faculty and staff engaging in data collection and provided feedback.

Team Member: "Well, I provided feedback to the staff when they didn't collect the data."

Does this scenario sound familiar? If you've worked in education long enough, you've likely heard different versions of the same complaint. This story is not uncommon. You know, grumblings like, "They aren't doing their job," "They aren't holding up their end," or "I told them what to do, and they still aren't doing it." We've all heard this and most likely have said it ourselves. Some even hurl adjectives such as "lazy," "useless," "weak," or perhaps "ridiculous" as frustration sets in when staff isn't performing as expected.

Soon fingers are pointed, feelings hurt, and nothing changes. And in some cases, large sums of money are dumped into training as the assumption is made that faculty and staff have not been trained properly. This cycle repeats itself in many schools across the country.

The irony is that in our eagerness to bring out the best in our students, we forget the importance of bringing out the best in our faculty and staff. And when folks aren't performing well, we tend to lose our way as we blame, complain, and continue on the hamster wheel of resentment instead of seeking to support staff performance.

One of the roles of a school leader should be to identify why faculty or staff are performing poorly and intervene to ensure performance is improved. When faculty or staff aren't performing (e.g., a behavior tech isn't running a plan correctly; a teacher isn't instructing students effectively), there is always a reason beyond "lazy" or any of the choice adjectives above. Simply put, they either can't do it or won't do it. More accurately, there is either a skill deficit or a performance deficit.

But how does a school leader determine this without painstaking and time-consuming assessments? Don't despair! Organizational Behavior Management (OBM) practitioners have already developed a simple tool that can help. This tool, known as the Performance Diagnostic Checklist–Human Services (PDC-HS) (Carr et al., 2013), contains a series of simple questions that can be used to determine the ultimate root cause of performance issues.

You might think about the PDC as the functional behavior assessment (FBA) of performance management, where the FBA tells us why misbehavior occurs, and the PDC tells us why employee performance *is not improving*.

And here is the best part: The assessment comes with built-in recommendations for several evidence-/function-based interventions for improving faculty and staff performance. Specifically, the Intervention Planning section provides appropriate interventions in the four areas assessed, including (a) training, (b) task clarification and prompting (c) resources, materials, and processes, and (d) performance consequences, effort, and competition (Carr et al., 2013).

After discovering the value of the PDC, we introduced the tool to many school leaders and colleagues who quickly adopted it. When we observe performance issues, we immediately begin viewing them through a PDC lens. Rather than blame the faculty or staff, we search for root causes of performance issues using this tool.

These questions help you diagnose the reason behind any performance gap linked to Parts 1 and 2 of the QuickWOC tool. Often, leaders are aware of a problem but are unsure how to approach it. Moreover, some leaders try to fix different problems using the same approach. This can result in disaster when it comes to performance issues!

The questions in the PDC originated from the work of Dr. John Austin (Austin, 2000), who created the tool for diagnosing performance issues. The PDC shown in *Quick Wins* is adapted from the original and modified for use by school leaders. The PDC is an interview-based assessment methodology covering four performance areas often at the root of a performance gap. These areas are:

Antecedents and Information: These either set the stage or are "triggers" for people's behavior. Examples include policies and procedures, job aids, teacher evaluation guidelines, academic and daily schedules, training, announcements, etc.

Equipment and Processes: These are the tools, technology, and procedures to support behavior. Examples include computers, school supplies for students and teachers, walking path signage, etc.

Knowledge and Skills—Training: These are the specific knowledge and skills needed to perform the behavior. Examples include teacher in-service training, teacher and student evaluation categories, and district personnel instructional coaching and mentoring.

Motivation: Originally titled *Consequences,* this consists of the outcomes of performing the behavior—what the individual experiences as a result. Examples include praise to teachers and students in the hallways, public recognition for academic achievement, and disciplinary action for misbehavior or violating school policy. For students, this might mean suspension, while for educators, it might mean disciplinary action for violating the code of ethics.

Generally, the PDC is used by administrators with employees— specifically, subject matter experts (SMEs) who can provide enough depth for analyzing the performance gap. In large systems or districts with multiple sites, it can be delivered using a sampling approach (e.g., selecting a couple of teachers from each grade level) to avoid taking a great deal of time.

The PDC can and should be used in conjunction with direct observations to support the validity of the results. Because of this last point, we recommend using the PDC only *after* completing Parts 1 and 2 of QuickWOC. At this point, the school leaders have conducted their walkabouts, gathered additional insight from other support professionals, and can now diagnose the problem before implementing the Quick Win.

Part 3—The Performance Diagnostic Checklist

Specify a behavior you need to improve based on Parts 1 and 2 of QuickWOC. Walk through the questions from the viewpoint of the person performing the behavior. Identify a solution for any "No" response; the solution may be a Quick Win.

Antecedents and Information	YES	NO
1. Is there a written description stating the clear expectation of the educator regarding a particular instructional/behavioral strategy?		
2. Has the educator received adequate instruction about what to do (e.g., instructions such as "I want you to do this and this before we leave today")?		

Antecedents and Information	YES	NO

3. Has the educator received formal training on this instructional/behavioral strategy?

   If yes, check all applicable training methods.

   ☐ Instructions   ☐ Demonstration   ☐ Rehearsal

4. Is there a task aid visible **while** completing the instructional/behavioral strategy in question (e.g., reminders to prompt the strategy correctly at the right time/duration)?

5. Can the educator state the purpose of the instructional/ behavioral strategy?

6. Is the educator verbally, textually, or electronically reminded to use the instructional/behavioral strategy?
   If yes, how often?

   ☐ Hourly   ☐ Daily   ☐ Weekly   ☐ Monthly

   By whom? Check all that apply:

   ☐ Peer   ☐ Coach   ☐ Administrator   ☐ Other

7. Are there frequently updated, challenging, and attainable goals the educator is comfortable with about the instructional/ behavioral strategy?

8. Is the educator "aware" of the school's mission?

Equipment and Processes	YES	NO

9. If equipment is required, is it available and in good working order (e.g., computer, A/V, mic, etc.)?

10. Are the equipment and environment optimally arranged in a physical sense (e.g., the arrangement of the students' desks)?

11. Are larger processes performing well despite incorrect instructional/ behavioral strategies (e.g., routines and procedures)?

12. Are these processes written out and arranged logically?

13. Can the educator implement the instructional/behavioral strategy without any obstacles (e.g., interruption by the intercom)?

Knowledge and Skills–Training	YES	NO
14. Can the educator tell you what they are supposed to be doing and how to do it?		
15. Can the educator physically/verbally precisely demonstrate the instructional/behavioral strategy?		
16. If the instructional/behavioral strategy needs to be completed quickly, can the educator perform it at the appropriate speed?		

Motivation	YES	NO
17. Are educators motivated based on the outcomes following the completion of the task?		
18. Do educators see the positive effects of implementing the instructional/behavioral strategy (e.g., increased student engagement, increased assessment data, decreased misbehavior)?		
19. Do administrators monitor the educator's behavior related to the task? If yes, how often? ☐ Hourly ☐ Daily ☐ Weekly ☐ Monthly		
20. Does the educator receive feedback about their performance? If yes, By whom? _____ and How often? ☐ Hourly ☐ Daily ☐ Weekly ☐ Monthly How long of a delay between observing the instructional/behavioral strategy and delivering feedback? _____ Check all that apply: Feedback Focus: ☐ Positive ☐ Constructive Feedback Type: ☐ Written ☐ Verbal ☐ Graphed ☐ Other		
21. Is the instructional/behavioral strategy easy to implement?		
22. Do other instructional/behavioral strategies appear to take precedence over the targeted strategy?		

Quick Takeaways:

- Evaluate Quick Win opportunities based on their impact, visibility, and effort.

- The Quick Win Matrix gives you a visual tool for prioritizing Quick Wins. The higher the impact and the lower the effort, the better the Quick Win. The target change must hold high-impact value and be highly visible, with a low response effort.

- Identifying Quick Wins should be a *quick* process. The first step in identifying Quick Wins requires walking around, making direct observations, and conversing with people throughout the school.

- The QuickWOC observation form is divided into seven domains that ask questions about the most visible common areas of the school. The areas identified are typically problematic during a school turnaround.

- The QuickWOC tool is designed to use some key common areas in the school during a walkthrough to identify Quick Wins to target for change.

- A QuickWOC involves three parts:

  ◦ Part 1—Walkabout Observations: This is a walking tour of school facilities. The observation team can be administrators, teachers, students, and other key stakeholders.

  ◦ Part 2—Other Sources: Gather other sources of information and data to potential Quick Wins. These data can be obtained from meetings, interviews, and focus groups. The principal and leadership team may also analyze other data types during this process, such as climate and discipline data.

  ◦ Part 3—Performance Diagnostic Checklist: Use the PDC to determine the root cause of performance issues.

- People tend to be poor observers of their behavior, the impact on the environment, and the impact of the environment on their behavior.

Sustain It:

- Why might stakeholders resist change when identifying Quick Wins? What are some ways to minimize the resistance?

- What are some ways to support stakeholders through turnaround change efforts?

- The PDC is an excellent tool for diagnosing performance issues. In what other ways might you use the PDC to help an individual be a better observer of their behavior?

CHAPTER 5:

Quick Wins Require
IMPACT Goals and Data

After completing the three-step QuickWOC process to target Quick Wins, which includes observations, information gathering from stakeholders, analysis of pertinent data, and performance diagnostics, it's time to set goals.

Traditionally, S.M.A.R.T. goals (Doran, 1981), which stands for Specific, Measurable, Achievable, Relevant, and Time-bound, have been the go-to in education. And while they have their strengths, it is our contention that they leave out critical variables necessary to increase the likelihood that goals will be accomplished. We like to use *IMPACT Goals.*

IMPACT Goals

Goals should give leaders and school staff a clear destination and let them adjust the course as needed. IMPACT Goals are:

- Individualized

- Manageable

- Positively motivating

- Aligned

- Connected

- Trackable

Let's take a look at each element:

INDIVIDUALIZED. Rather than being general, the goal is stated precisely in terms of what the desired result is. In addition, the goal is specific to the needs of the individual or group required to achieve them. Individually or collectively, people need goals relevant to their roles and responsibilities. For example, if a teacher is struggling with behavioral challenges across the classroom that interfere with instruction and student achievement, then focusing on classroom management would likely be very specific to the teacher's needs.

- Does the goal state precisely what the desired result is?
- Is the goal specific to the needs of the stakeholder(s)?
- Is the goal relevant to the roles and responsibilities of the stakeholder(s)?

MANAGEABLE. To accomplish goals, people need the knowledge, skills, and resources to be successful. In addition, they can't have too many goals thrown at them at once; otherwise, achieving them is unmanageable. As the old saying goes, *nothing is important if everything is important.* Therefore, providing stakeholders with knowledge, skills, and resources aimed at just a couple of goals at a time is far more likely to have an impact than attempting to focus on a bunch of goals at once.

- Do staff have the knowledge and skills to reach this goal?
- Are resources provided to support those who need to implement or engage in the change (time, tools, money, authority, etc.)?
- Are there a few goals focused on at a time?

POSITIVELY MOTIVATING. The highest IMPACT Goal is motivating stakeholders. We are not only talking about self-sustaining motivation, where people are energized simply by the nature of the goal. We are also talking about *leaders' actions* to motivate people to engage in the change. Leaders should solicit feedback and involve people in goal setting and planning as a powerful source of motivation. They should then deliberately look for opportunities to reinforce incremental improvement to keep performance moving toward goals positively. The goal needs to be something that stakeholder(s) find value in achieving. For example, in the classroom management scenario, if behavioral challenges occur because teachers report they aren't trained in managing problem behavior, then developing a classroom management plan would likely be a positive, motivating goal.

- Why should stakeholders engage in the change?
- How will feedback be solicited?
- How will behavior be positively reinforced?
- How will we celebrate the success of the Quick Win?

ALIGNED. Goals do not achieve themselves—they require appropriate behavior. Therefore, IMPACT Goals link to the behaviors faculty and staff must engage in to achieve the goal as part of their day-to-day work. For example, an aligned IMPACT Goal for improving class-wide behavior in a classroom where behavioral challenges are prominent would be to ensure faculty and staff engage in classroom management strategies taught during training. These might be teaching expectations, observing students, positively reinforcing expected behavior, and quietly and consistently correcting behaviors not aligned with the classroom management expectations. Engaging in the behaviors consistently impacts everybody in the classroom, as more teaching and learning occur when behavioral challenges are minimal.

- Have the specific behaviors required to achieve the goals been identified?

- Is the change outlined and described specifically in the roles and responsibilities of those who will need to change?

- Is this change adding value for the students, teachers, and staff?

CONNECTED. This means shifting from looking at achieving long-term results or the end goal to focus on shorter accomplishments. We will unpack accomplishments in a later chapter but, in short, accomplishments are the shorter-term outcomes of behavior that serve as a salient measure of progress toward IMPACT Goals. In the classroom management example, this might be a written classroom management plan, the number of expectations posted, and the number of students who can state expectations. These link to the goal of improving class-wide behavior through classroom management. Whether at the individual or group level, the accomplishments describe what the school needs to do to be successful, as they link people's actions to valued results.

- What accomplishments need to occur for the individual, group, or school to be successful?

- Are the accomplishments aligned with behavior?

- Which of these accomplishments will serve as salient measures of progress toward goals?

TRACKABLE. What gets measured moves. For a goal to be measured, it should be described in clear, unambiguous terms and include details of how it will be measured, tracked, and evaluated. A specific goal with a progress monitoring process clearly outlined has a much greater chance of being accomplished because it precisely describes what you are looking to change, at what intervals you will be measuring that change, and what data will measure it. The most effective IMPACT Goals include behavior metrics and are sorted into leading and lagging indicators in the form of accomplishments and subgoals, which we'll unpack in a later chapter. For example, a general goal identified by leadership at a school might be to "improve school-wide discipline," but a trackable IMPACT Goal is specific and outlined starting with the end in mind.

- Are short-term goals (targets) established for the Quick Win?

- Does your school employ database systems to reinforce progress toward school academic and climate goals?

- Does your school have ongoing measures for climate and student/teacher efficacy?

Let's take an example of a trackable IMPACT Goal at the school level:

- Goal: Reduce discipline referrals by 20% by implementing classroom management strategies within 60 days

- Subgoal: Reduce discipline referrals by 5%

Accomplishments:

- The number of faculty and staff trained

- The number of faculty and staff who have completed classroom management plans

- The number of faculty who have expectations posted

- The number of faculty who have taught classroom management expectations

- The number of students who can state expectations

The importance of developing IMPACT Goals can't be overstated. Detailed planning drastically increases the likelihood that the school will achieve its goals. To aid you in creating goals with the highest IMPACT, we provide a checklist in the Appendix to guide you. Let's dive deeper into the IMPACT Goals. We'll give more examples at the school level for achieving Quick Wins.

IMPACT Goals and Data, Data, Data!

After identifying your IMPACT Goals, data are essential to manage and celebrate Quick Wins. You might be thinking, "They're talking data again. We don't have time for that. We need action *right now!*"

Although "data" may often be thought of as a dirty four-letter word, data are your friend—you can use them to help achieve Quick Wins and help your school grow. The fact is: you don't have time *not* to collect data. Like a football scoreboard, these data allow you to *see* your progress or lack thereof. Good data let you observe even the smallest changes.

When things are going well, school leaders should reinforce student and staff behavior for even the slightest changes (remember, this is called "shaping" in the behavioral sciences). Use the data to adjust your game plan if things aren't going well. For example, suppose you are considering implementing a Quick Win and approaching a natural school break (e.g., winter break). In that case, you can collect data before the break (about 3 days' worth should be adequate) and implement your strategic plan immediately following the holiday. The "now" data can be used as a baseline later.

Using data does not have to be complicated. You can—and should—create your way of measuring your Quick Wins. You might think, "I don't have the time or the knowledge to create metrics." That's understandable, given technological advancements and complicated, expensive measurement systems. Folks marvel at these systems' ability, but districts and schools frequently lack the money to purchase them or possess the patience and desire to learn how to use them efficiently. However, most schools have a tool or program for counting something (e.g., number of students, grades, attendance, teacher vacation days, etc.) that could be leveraged to collect your needed data.

However, if the school or district doesn't have a way to capture the needed data, you can create *your own* "scoreboard" to illustrate progress on a few IMPACT Goals. Once you've completed your IMPACT Goals, selecting and creating your data measures should be simple. It's essentially like creating a road map to get to a destination. When you do this, you can identify some metrics that serve as leading and lagging indicators.

Leading and Lagging Indicators—Metrics

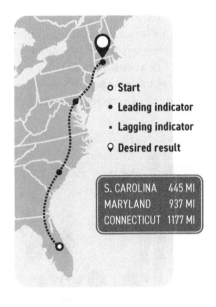

FIGURE 5.1: Start with the desired end result in mind, and then identify leading and lagging indicators as measures of progress towards the end result. A leading indicator is a metric that looks at the here and now to determine if you are moving in the right direction. A lagging indicator looks back at whether the intended progress toward the end result was achieved.

o Start

• Leading indicator

· Lagging indicator

♀ Desired result

S. CAROLINA   445 MI
MARYLAND   937 MI
CONNECTICUT   1177 MI

Many people confuse the notion of leading and lagging indicators. But we like to keep things simple by applying concepts to everyday life when needed. For example, perhaps you live in Florida and decide to visit your family in Connecticut for the holidays. You determine it will take 3 days to reach them (goal) by driving your favorite scenic route (behavior). Along the way, mile markers and signs are leading indicators to let you know you are headed in the right direction. Crossing state lines within X amount of time lets you know that you are staying on course with your goal of reaching your family in 3 days. See?—not as difficult as it sounds!

Teachers use leading and lagging indicators in the form of informal formative assessments, quizzes, tests, benchmarks, etc. These metrics help guide instruction and, collectively, help school leaders predict student achievement and make adjustments as necessary.

Regarding discipline challenges, the number of students sent out of the classroom daily might be a leading indicator of the number of suspensions that occur in a month. Depending on the time frame being assessed, other leading and lagging indicators might be attendance, climate surveys, parent complaints, student reassignments, etc. Because data are important for achieving Quick Wins and sustainability with any IMPACT Goal, let's dig into this concept further.

The Value of Leading Indicators

After identifying Quick Wins and creating IMPACT Goals, you'll want to determine some metrics. Determine what you'll measure and divide them into leading and lagging indicators:

LEADING INDICATORS: *What you are seeing now* to let you know you are on the right track. Think about them as a way to look forward and predict future outcomes.

LAGGING INDICATORS: *What has happened.* While they are still a predictor of the future, if you stay on the same path, think about them as a way to look back to figure out how you got here.

LEADING INDICATORS ARE RELATED TO STUDENT BEHAVIOR AND STAFF PERFORMANCE. If you remember, one of the Quick Wins Principal Daniels tackled as a goal was related to the cafeteria. Leading indicators in this setting might

FIGURE 5.2: Divide the cafeteria into sections with designated staff assigned to each one.

be measures such as the number of students in their seats, the number of students put on time-out, the number of staff at their posts, or the frequency of adult-to-student interaction (The recommended ratio of positive to negative interactions is 4:1). Collecting these data can be simple. You might divide the cafeteria into a grid and observe different areas for 10 minutes while using pencil-and-paper to record incidents of student behavior and frequency of staff behavior. Repeat this process during different lunch times. *(See Figure 5.2.)*

LAGGING INDICATORS ARE OUTCOMES THAT THESE LEADING INDI-CATORS WILL IMPACT. Lagging data include discipline referrals and social valid-ity measures (i.e., staff perceptions) relating to the cafeteria. For example, suppose Principal Daniels and his team looked at office discipline referrals at the end of the week, and the data indicated they were down. In that case, they could reflect on precisely what happened to produce this outcome and consider refining their pro-cesses for the next week if they want to make even more progress.

We will dive deeper into Principal Daniels's approach to handling the caf-eteria later as we illustrate Quick Wins. But for now, we hope you see the value of looking at data. Not just student achievement data but any sort of data that put you in a position to positively reinforce the improvement and help you determine if you are moving in the right direction. Let's take a look at the use of IMPACT Goals and QuickWOCs. Remember, QuickWOCs allow you to collect real data for determining Quick Wins. *(See Figure 5.3.)*

Quick Wins for Moving Toward Goals

An excellent Quick Win for keeping faculty and staff motivated and moving toward established goals is to shift from looking at achieving long-term results to shorter-term accomplishments. A source of leading and lagging indica-tors, accomplishments serve as salient measures of progress toward IMPACT Goals. For example, if you aim to reduce suspensions by 50%, you might break that down into subgoals of 10% increments. For instance:

- Subgoal 1: 10%

- Subgoal 2: 20%

- Subgoal 3: 30%

- Subgoal 4: 40%

- Goal: 50%

FIGURE 5.3: Create subgoals and then identify accomplishments as salient measures toward IMPACT Goals.

You might then identify a series of accomplishments that will move faculty and staff toward the subgoals. Principal Daniels noticed behavioral challenges in the hallways and classrooms. As such, accomplishments might be measured as:

- The number of faculty and staff at their post in the morning

- The number of faculty who have created classroom management plans

- The number of teachers who have taught the expectations associated with the classroom management plans

- The number of students who can state the expectations

Almost like a master checklist, as these accomplishments are progressively checked off (e.g., all faculty have classroom management plans, all faculty and staff are at their assigned posts), you, as a school leader are in a position to positively reinforce their progress. Much like a GPS, accomplishments do a much better job of letting both leadership and the performer know they are moving in the right direction. In Chapter 4 we covered QuickWOCs. Now let's connect IMPACT Goals with potential Quick Wins that may have been identified during the QuickWOC assessment.

Examples of Using IMPACT Goals and QuickWOCs for Achieving Quick Wins

DIRTY, DINGY HALLWAYS

QUICKWOC ASSESSMENT AND RATIONALE: Ten dirty, dingy hallways and the school entrance need painting. These hallways could give parents and students the impression that staff is not "invested" in the school.

IMPACT GOAL: To improve the appearance of the hallways, schedule the maintenance team to paint the ten hallways and the school's entrance before students and staff return. A nonspecific goal might just say, "Paint the hallways."

DATA MEASURES AND FEEDBACK: Use a checklist for the ten hallways and the entrance. All stakeholders can see changes themselves, and school leaders will provide feedback to staff.

MORNING FIGHTS

QUICKWOC ASSESSMENT AND RATIONALE: Discipline data indicate frequent morning fights in the cafeteria. Staff interviews reveal no current expectations for students or staff.

IMPACT GOAL: Develop cafeteria procedures at the first discipline team meeting, then train cafeteria staff in these procedures on the first in-service day.

A non-achievable goal might be to require more staff in the cafeteria in a school that already has staffing issues.

Data Measures and Feedback: Use sign-in sheets for training.

Collect discipline data at the end of 2 weeks to measure student behavior. During the first week, observe each staff member with a checklist of critical behaviors (supervise the area, praise students, give students time-out for misbehavior).

LONG LINES

QuickWOC Assessment and Rationale: Lunch staff complains of long lines, and students complain they lack time to eat lunch. Directly observing the arrival of classes at the cafeteria reveals that 16 of 20 classes were late. The observation indicated that all clocks across the school needed to be synchronized.

IMPACT Goal: Immediately schedule maintenance to synchronize clocks. Send an email to solicit feedback on any existing barriers to punctuality. Share finalized schedule with staff. Give a raffle ticket to teachers who arrive within a 2-minute window. While it's easy to track staff arrival after syncing clocks, collecting baseline data before the intervention allows for tracking and reinforcement of improvements.

Data Measures and Feedback: Use the existing schedule to mark the arrival of classes on time. Give the teacher a raffle ticket and thank them for arriving on time.

Email staff noting any improvements in punctuality (e.g., "We've gone from 20% punctuality to 80% in just 1 day. You guys are the best!").

Email all staff noting improvements during lunchtime resulting from changes.

IMPACT Goals in Action

When it comes to IMPACT Goals, here are five important things to consider. Each can potentially make or break your turnaround:

1. What do you want people to do more of, less of, or differently?

2. What measures indicate movement, telling you the turnaround is working? What "leading indicators" will tell the story?

3. What tools will you use to collect data, and who will collect, report, and review it?

4. Once you've selected your measures, whom will you designate to create a simple "scoreboard" to share regularly with staff?

5. When you initiate change, present measures of progress to the targeted staff at least weekly, no less than monthly.

Let's unpack each of these even further.

Consideration #1: What do you want people to do more of, less of, or differently? Determine the results you desire related to the school's ultimate goals and define staff behaviors that align with these ultimate goals.

It is important to be precise here. For example, we once asked staff to focus more on students transitioning to class during morning arrival by standing at key places and providing "positive attention" to students as they entered the school. However, during our first-morning observation, we realized that our emphasis on "positive attention" inadvertently encouraged staff to ignore misbehavior. As students ran by, staff simply said, "Good morning"!

To remedy this, we had a 5-minute meeting prior to school starting the next day. We acknowledged our failure to be specific and reminded staff to not only increase focus on positive interactions but consistently correct misbehavior as well. We modeled what positive interactions should look like and then gave an example of the most common misbehavior at the time (running) and how to correct it. Remember the correction strategy Principal Daniels used at Hawkins Heights to correct the students' running behavior in the hallway? When students ran in the hallway, we instructed the staff to have the students walk back from where they began running. Using the walk-back correction quickly eliminated the students from running in the halls!

CONSIDERATION #2: WHAT MEASURES WILL INDICATE MOVEMENT, TELLING YOU THE TURNAROUND IS WORKING? WHAT "LEADING INDICATORS" WILL TELL THE STORY? These can include staff and student perception (e.g., climate surveys), staff and student attendance, staff timeliness to duties, counts of positive to negative interactions, and discipline data (Supovitz et al., 2012). Whatever data measures you select should tell the story of the turnaround. Is it working? Are you moving toward the right result?

CONSIDERATION #3: WHAT TOOLS WILL YOU USE TO COLLECT DATA, AND WHO WILL COLLECT, REPORT, AND REVIEW THEM? These tools may already be in place for data on discipline, attendance, student performance, etc. In the case of specific behaviors, a simple pencil-and-paper checklist can serve you well. For example, imagine simply asking one of your staff on duty during dismissal to tally how many students were running to the bus. Or ask an instructional coach to count how often students called out during whole-group instruction.

Remember, when discussing behavior, we are not only discussing student behavior. You need to count teacher behavior as well. In the example of students calling out, a principal might count how many times a teacher used correction versus how many times praise was used.

While these measures are critical to a successful turnaround, they can also be critical for demonstrating to staff that the Quick Wins are working and that the turnaround is happening in incremental steps versus waiting for an end result.

CONSIDERATION #4: ONCE YOU'VE SELECTED YOUR MEASURES, WHOM WILL YOU DESIGNATE TO CREATE A SIMPLE "SCOREBOARD" TO SHARE REGULARLY WITH STAFF? You might choose a designee for each measure. For example, discipline data might be collected and made into a presentable form by the school's psychologist, achievement data by the school's assistant principal, and student or teacher attendance data by the school's secretary.

Whatever method you use, list three-to-five data measures with targets set on some timetable (weekly, monthly, quarterly). But beware, just collecting data isn't enough. Once it's collected, stakeholders need to see it!

CONSIDERATION #5: WHEN YOU INITIATE CHANGE, WE HIGHLY RECOMMEND PRESENTING MEASURES OF PROGRESS TO THE TARGETED STAFF AT LEAST WEEKLY, NO LESS THAN MONTHLY. Just as a sports team needs to know the score and where they are on the field ASAP to reinforce or adjust plays, your school team needs to be fed back measures quickly. In other words, it's not enough to just collect data. These measures need to be presented in a quick and easy-to-understand format so the feedback can be acted upon as required.

For example, let's say that student discipline referrals are down 15% after 1 week as a result of a new behavior support program. Teachers given these data are likely to feel empowered by the evidence of steady improvement. Simply seeing meaningful outcomes can have a powerful impact on performance. In another example, at the leadership team level, showing the leadership members' staff absenteeism or a climate survey at the end of a month could demonstrate the impact of their support.

You can be creative in the data presentation and link it to your school theme. Make it fun! Data might be presented as multiple graphs posted in a weekly newsletter or common area where all staff can regularly view it. Or it can be posted on something that looks like a scoreboard. (More on visual feedback later.)

Figure 5.4 is an example of how one school graphically showed the total number of "codes called in" (requests for assistance) to the administration (Gavoni et al., 2017). Three codes described various behavior problems, and one indicated a medical emergency. The data were collected and graphed to show teachers and administrators how the codes were used to monitor behavior over time.

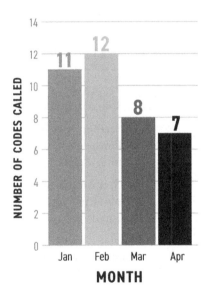

Codes Called in Cafeteria by Month

FIGURE 5.4: Codes called in the cafeteria by month. (Codes were: 1 = continuous aggression and/or self-injury observed; 2 = continuous high-magnitude disruption and/or property disruption; 3 = student out of the assigned area; blue = medical emergency.) Adapted from Gavoni et al. (2017).

Once again, data can be used in a variety of ways. They can be used to: reinforce the current approach based on staff's perceptions; adjust the current system; communicate with the staff about any misperceptions discovered through the data analysis; and many more.

Quick Takeaways:

- Data analysis is integral to managing and celebrating Quick Wins. Meaningful data allow you to observe even small changes in behavior. Positively reinforcing successful approximations or small steps toward a goal is called shaping.

- All data are not equal. You must collect the "correct" data relevant to the change initiative.

- Using data does not have to be complicated. Create a specialized data collection system that meets your needs for analyzing Quick Wins progress.

- Leading and lagging indicators are just metrics. Leading indicators tell what is happening now, informing an organization that they are on the right track. Lagging indicators tell an organization what has happened in the past.

- Five critical considerations with IMPACT Goals during a school turnaround:

  1. Determine precisely what results you want relating to the school's ultimate goals, then define staff behaviors to align with the school's ultimate goals.

  2. Select data measures that tell the story of the turnaround. Your data should tell you what's working and if you're moving toward the desired result.

  3. Data collection is a critical element to a successful turnaround. Determine the methods of collecting the data needed and who will be responsible for managing the data.

  4. Consider how often the data are reviewed and shared with stakeholders.

  5. Share the data with stakeholders! List three-to-five data measures with targets set on a timetable (weekly, monthly, quarterly). Create a "scoreboard" for the public posting of data.

Sustain It:

- Use the QuickWOCs process to develop IMPACT Goals for the identified Quick Wins. Now that you've identified 2–3 Quick Wins from the QuickWOC process, create goals for each using the IMPACT Goal format. Remember, IMPACT Goals are individualized, manageable, positively motivating, aligned, connected, and trackable.

Use this format:

1. Identified Quick Win

2. QuickWOC Assessment and Rationale

3. IMPACT Goal–Data Measures and Feedback

- From the IMPACT Goals you've created, identify some critical leading and lagging indicators to measure. Remember, accomplishments serve as salient measures of progress toward IMPACT Goals.

CHAPTER 6:

Quick Wins Require Communication

"And words are, of course, the most powerful drug used by humankind."

— Rudyard Kipling in his 1923 address to the Royal College of
Surgeons in London

The capacity of communication to make or break any change cannot be over-stated. "Sticks and stones may break my bones, but words will never hurt me," rings hollow within school hallways. Yet, words *can* break morale, effort, momen-tum, relationships, and achievement. *What, when, and how* a leader communicates is powerful and can make or break a school.

When used positively, words can motivate, strengthen, and build a school that can positively impact generations of families—and positively impact the world because of the fundamental importance of education to the lives of students and civil societies.

Effective communication is essential for all leaders who seek to bring out the best in their staff within any organization. In schools, communication rep-resents the core of strengthening relationships, improving performance, and fos-tering self-efficacy in ways that help students achieve. Given the unequivocal power of communication, it is a shame that more educational leadership preparation pro-grams need to provide greater focus in this area.

Communication is very complex, as it entails a combination of body lan-guage, tone of voice, timing, and content. Even with the complexities of commu-nication, simple strategies can have a profound, positive, and lasting effect on staff behavior and morale when used correctly and in the right way. There are things a leader can say and cannot "unsay."

School leaders must be aware that their communication is under constant scrutiny. Each time a leader effectively communicates, it is comparable to a deposit in the "relationship bank." However, each time a leader is ineffective in commu-nication, it is like making a withdrawal. And what happens when you withdraw more money than you've deposited in your bank? Overdraft fees!

In the context of school improvement, "overdraft fees" can manifest in a "negative balance" that includes a lack of motivation, reduced trust in the administration, and the development of a negative climate. While specific well-timed communication strategies can lead to significant deposits, one poorly timed, ineffective communication attempt can stall a turnaround or even sink it for good.

The turnaround process is a fragile endeavor, and communication blunders during the early stages can have a negative effect that is multiplied. We've seen well-meaning leaders err during the critical launch, never to recover. Staff quickly lose faith in such a leader and mistrust and dislike the person. *(Warning! If your staff does not like you, your attempts at communication will likely lose the desired impact. Even strategies like praise will not be positively received.)*

Our relationship-bank analogy is affirmed by Aubrey Daniels (2016, p. 164) who emphatically states, "to make reinforcement, reward, and recognition effective, you must first develop good relationships with people."

Seven Communication Strategies for Quick Wins

Do you need help communicating or developing relationships? If so, or if you want to improve your communication to strengthen relationships further, try the following communication strategies below. The techniques help build leaders who are effective communicators who are well-liked and who inspire staff to go above and beyond.

These communication strategies foster collective self-efficacy and create a phenomenon called "positive emotional contagion" (Kramer et al., 2014). It is characterized by the spreading contented staff perception and the optimistic feeling and productive behaviors that typify contented people. We categorize these communication strategies as Quick Wins because they are!

Communication Quick Win #1—Using the Power of Persuasion

As a school leader, your position enables you to leverage the power of persuasion. With the know-how to persuade through effective communication, you can forge relationships essential to ensuring that Quick Wins are implemented. In *From Good Schools to Great Schools: What Their Principals Do Well*, authors Gray and Streshly compare traits of principals and corporate leaders, including qualities exclusive to school leadership. The authors eloquently share how "school leaders matter because they have the clout to mold the conversation, the topic, and how the topic is talked about" (Gray & Streshly, 2008, p. 15).

School leaders influence to bring people within a school together and to shape the culture. This is separate from simply telling folks what to do. The idea is to provide a framework of collaboration to shape a community toward caring and mutual learning that permeates throughout the school. This learning occurs through two primary sources: positive and constructive feedback. Positive feedback is specific information intended to reinforce teacher or staff behavior by letting them know exactly what they are doing correctly. Constructive feedback is specific information intended to help the teacher or staff do something more, less, or differently. Both types of feedback are intended to help people in regard to performance goals.

Communication Quick Win #2—Delivering Performance-Based Feedback

The power of feedback to unlock the best performance is critical and often overlooked or underutilized. Performance feedback provides information that guides behavior in the right direction—from debating to making decisions, from fighting fires to strategic planning, and from directing to effective teaching.

Feedback encourages the correct behavior to happen. Without it, people need to guess how and what they are doing and, in the worst case, think they are doing all the right things when they may be doing all the wrong things. In turnaround schools, feedback is the most valuable behavior leaders can engage in to improve staff performance. The goal of performance feedback is simple: Help people perform to achieve results. By increasing or adding more performance-based feedback, leaders can immediately unlock a Quick Win toward accelerating and achieving performance goals during a turnaround.

For example, at one turnaround school, behavioral issues that once plagued the hallways were reduced to only minor ones. However, student achievement still stagnated. Some were calling it a "Happy-Crappy" school. After doing a walkabout and noting limited engagement between teachers and students, leaders determined that what would have the largest impact on achievement would be to increase student engagement. Specifically, this meant helping teachers engage their students by asking higher-order thinking questions at an increased rate.

After providing a brief in-service on a managing-response-rate technique (e.g., choral responding during whole-group activities), the principal would prompt the use of the response-rate technique. At the beginning of each day, before students arrived, she used the school's intercom to wish all staff a "good morning" and then reminded the teachers of the managing-response-rate strategy to focus on during the week. By doing this, teachers knew what the leadership team would look for as they walked through classrooms. Moreover, the leadership team knew what to provide feedback on. As the leadership team walked through, they made quick notes regarding what teachers were doing well and what slight changes would help them improve further. Leadership put out an email highlighting exceptional managing-response-rate techniques observed, praised staff for their efforts, and then provided tips on improving further for those who were trying but still not implementing with fidelity. Leadership then repeated the process until almost all performed the technique precisely and celebrated success as student achievement began to grow.

Communication Quick Win #3—Reinforcing Progress Toward Subgoals

In OBM, a fundamental premise to achieve performance is using subgoals effectively. Subgoals are IMPACT Goals broken down into smaller goals. As mentioned in Chapter 5, you might then identify a series of accomplishments that will let folks know they are moving toward achieving the subgoals.

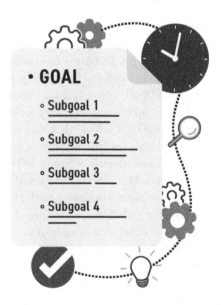

The path to achieving the ultimate end goal remains clear by reinforcing progress toward subgoals. Leaders can establish a Quick Win by setting frequent subgoals followed by frequent performance feedback and reinforcement. If the leader has targeted the right behaviors to reinforce, results are all but instantaneous.

It is not unusual for subgoals to be viewed as small changes and for most "small changes" to go unnoticed. By focusing on subgoals, the leader has implemented a communication Quick Win, enabling the leader to look for and reinforce those "small changes." It is a crucial role of leadership to illuminate even the smallest improvement during a school turnaround and provide feedback that aligns performance directly with it. Remember

FIGURE 6.1: Use subgoals as measures to provide more frequent performance feedback and reinforcement toward IMPACT Goals.

to identify accomplishments as leading and lagging indicators that let you and your stakeholders know whether things are moving in the right direction. When you hit those subgoals, remind and praise your stakeholders for their actions to accomplish them, then celebrate the success!

In the example of the managing-response-rate strategy illustrated above, a first subgoal might be to have at least 20% of teachers observed trying out the strategy. The next subgoal would be increased to 40%, and so on.

Communication Quick Win #4—Providing Feedback to Develop Self-Efficacy

You learned about self-efficacy in an earlier chapter, but it's worth revisiting in the classroom context. Instructional self-efficacy is a teacher's belief in their capacity to instruct effectively. It has been demonstrated to be a significant predictor of teacher and student success (Bandura, 1997). Self-efficacy reflects confidence in the teachers' ability to control their motivation, behavior, and social environment. Self-efficacy is not built magically. Evidence of success is needed to build self-efficacy and collective efficacy within a school, and feedback is essential for building efficacy.

Leaders implement a Quick Win that will last by focusing on feedback to develop self-efficacy. When people value doing something and believe they can do it, they have the ingredients required for success. As your staff accumulates successful experiences, their self-efficacy grows.

As a leader, it is your job to provide as much feedback as possible toward incremental improvement in their performance. However, it is not just about providing feedback but about providing it *strategically*. Seek to provide information that allows your staff to see where they stand against their own goals, not the goals or performance of others.

By focusing your feedback on a student's or teacher's performance related to their goals *and* delivering that feedback in a way that influences improvement, you are engaging the individual's confidence to perform—their self-efficacy.

Communication Quick Win #5—Strengthening Relationships Through Feedback

Leaders can use feedback to strengthen team relationships. During turnarounds, leaders must try to catch people doing things right. Finding these opportunities triggers leaders to give positive feedback up to four times as often as constructive feedback. Why?

Imagine a school where, whenever a teacher or student saw you, they turned around and walked the other way. The moment they see you, it triggers an emotional response: "Oh, it's him; better go the other way."

During school turnarounds, the health of relationships is critical to success. This may sound "fluffy" or "soft," but consider the results you are achieving under the conditions during the turnaround—people are already on edge, feeling emotions such as helplessness, being concerned, and possibly fearing for their jobs. You need to build and strengthen relationships with the team actively. Providing feedback, especially positive feedback, is a great way to do so.

Communication Quick Win #6—Using Constructive Feedback for Helping People Improve

It is not unusual for leaders to avoid confrontation. When this happens, they tend to allow subpar performance to occur, even in their presence. The contrary may be true in school turnarounds—when leaders deliver more constructive feedback, it helps to make the right things happen.

The problem is that this level and delivery of constructive feedback could be more constructive. It is negative, potentially damaging, and possibly hindering performance. You can deliver constructive feedback as a Quick Win to accelerate performance, but it is important to understand critical elements in genuinely constructive feedback.

DOING NOTHING IS DOING SOMETHING. Remember, we touched on this earlier. Not correcting performance is virtually condoning it! Imagine a student jogging down the hallways, passing multiple staff, as he rushes to the cafeteria for lunch. Assuming the hallway rules require students to walk, the staff's failure to correct the behavior will likely be seen as a go-ahead to jog. Other students may soon believe that jogging in the hallways to lunch is acceptable behavior; the next thing you know, the hallways feel like a track meet! (Doing *nothing* is doing *something*.)

The same goes for staff performance. We were in the cafeteria once and noticed lots of negative interaction as the monitoring staff constantly reprimanded students for speaking too loudly. The principal was present. The behavior management system required the staff to interact with students positively four times as often as they corrected misbehavior. Still, in this case, the interactions were closer to one positive to every ten negative. The principal never provided feedback to the staff. Her presence and failure to provide feedback *silently condoned the staff's behavior—and the students'*. (Doing *nothing* is doing *something*.) Help, not harm.

Corrective feedback should be constructive by nature to help the person perform better and should not be used as a means of confrontation or punishment. By delivering positive feedback four times more often than constructive feedback (what we call the 4:1 rule), your constructive feedback will be better received and more productive, and change can be observed to occur almost immediately.

However, suppose you address behavior when it fails to meet goals more than you recognize improvement. In that case, your communication may rapidly descend into the confrontation most people want to avoid.

In the example above, what might happen if the principal recognized each staff in the cafeteria when they provided a positive interaction with the students? Behavioral science tells us there is a good chance that these folks will begin providing more positive student interactions.

Unfortunately, when the principal fails to recognize any growth in staff and instead focuses on what they are *not* doing, pretty soon, staff are likely to become unhappy. They will even seek to avoid the principal.

DELIVER FEEDBACK IN PRIVATE. When providing corrective or constructive feedback, it is almost always best to do so privately. Nobody wants to be called out in public. Correcting performance in private shows staff respect and makes it more likely they will hear what you have to say instead of focusing on any embarrassment they feel.

FOCUS ON THE GOAL. Constructive feedback is about helping people. One sure way to do this is to focus on the goal. By reminding the individual of the goal, stating their performance in relation to the goal, and then giving them information to help them move toward that goal, success is more likely—faster and with better quality.

If you were helping a sprinter improve track time, you wouldn't get far if you just said, "improve your time." Instead, you would let them know their time in relation to the goal ("Your goal is 52 seconds; you ran that 400 in 60"), and then give them information to move them closer to that goal ("Don't forget to lengthen your stride off the turn").

Focusing on the goal gives you a double: It depersonalizes the feedback while providing information to help them perform better.

Communication Quick Win #7—Using Graphic Feedback to Strengthen Belief

It probably triggers a smile if you have ever invested money in the stock market and watched the Dow Jones graph steadily rise. Watching the graph rise gave you positive feedback, reinforcing your behavior to invest more and strengthening your self-efficacy (i.e., you believe yourself capable of accurately selecting profitable stocks). Nobody had to pat you on the back, tell you what a great job you did, or roll out a red carpet. Simply watching that little line move in a favorable trajectory gave you the feedback needed to maintain your course and strengthen your confidence, encouraging more and maybe riskier investments that might have big returns.

Graphs can be shared to show more than results. They can and should be shared as performance feedback, highlighting collective behaviors that led to the desired results. Remember, the ultimate goal of performance feedback is to help your staff grow in targeted skills. By aligning changes in targeted behaviors (e.g., using a new managing-response-rate technique) with improvement in meaningful results (such as increased student engagement, decreased disruptions, and increased academic achievement), even staff who are slow to engage in an initiative will take note and embrace the change. This can occur through timely, targeted graphic feedback of group data.

Have a Positive IMPACT With Data!

A principal once caught wind of how we used staff performance and results graphs. Feeling a need for change, she promptly had her leadership team do a walkthrough to collect data on a strategy her teachers were "trained" to use 2 months prior in their daily instruction. Once all data were collected, she posted it along with the results: Fewer than 5% of the teachers were using the strategy!

As you can imagine, the teacher's union was inundated with complaints to the school, and the principal was promptly (and incorrectly, in our opinion) reprimanded by union representatives. Did this make her a bad principal? Absolutely not! She intended to motivate staff through the use of these metrics.

However, she should have included a couple of essential things. The first was to collect baseline data, completing observations before the training to see where performance was pre-training. Because the teachers had been trained 2 months before, that initial walkthrough where only 5% of the staff performed the skill could have been kept as the baseline. You have to know where you are (baseline) before moving toward where you want to be (your goal).

Second, the principal should have informed the teachers of the leadership focus on collecting data on the new targeted behavior. The knowledge of the leader's commitment would serve as a trigger to the staff. They would know what the leadership would be looking for and reinforcing. People need to know what is expected and anticipate what will be reinforced to achieve the goal.

Let's revisit informing staff about a leader's intent to observe and collect data. Some argue that the act of informing will cause behavior to happen, regardless of observations and collecting data. And this is correct. When employees know that leaders will show up, take data, give feedback, and provide reinforcement, this will make the behavior happen. In fact, during turnarounds, this approach has never failed—every time staff was informed, the desired behavior happened! Is that a bad thing? No, of course not, that's the point. The goal is to get the staff to try the skills in a way that provides ample reinforcement.

By demonstrating the skills, leaders have one thing to do—provide positive reinforcement. If the principal had done this, she would have had a baseline and newly collected data. Even if the improvement is not vast, the leader still is in a position to reinforce the improvement. A simple picture or graph in an email with a brief note saying, "I'm proud of you! We are moving in the right direction!" can be enough to reinforce performance. Incidentally, when it comes to publicly shared graphed data, the focus should not be on the behavior of individuals but rather on the performance or results of a group (e.g., whole school, grade group). Individual data are almost always best shared in private, *especially* when it is indicating poor performance or results.

This process should be in every leader's toolkit during a turnaround and repeated throughout the turnaround:

1. Specifically, define behavior: What do you want people to do?

2. Get a baseline: Discover where the performance is.

3. Observe and measure: Take notes, find out if anything is getting in the way of performance, and take care of it.

4. Watch the performance happen and provide positive feedback.

5. Reinforce using graphic and verbal feedback until the skill is being performed at an acceptable level.

Graphic feedback is a simple and powerful tool for influencing behavior. Graphing progress is a very efficient and highly effective means of motivating staff. When goals are set, graphics help staff to easily discern where they are with respect to reaching the goals. When educators value the goal and have sufficient self-efficacy to believe they can meet the goal, a graph provides strong reinforcement toward achieving the turnaround.

Quick Takeaways:

- How a leader communicates is powerful and can make or break a school. Effective communication is essential for all leaders who seek to bring out the best in their staff within any organization.

- Communication can have a profound, positive, and lasting effect on staff behavior and morale when used at the right time and in the right way.

- Effective communication is like depositing in the "relationship bank." Each instance of ineffective communication is like making a withdrawal.

- Staff quickly lose faith in, mistrust, and dislike a leader who does not communicate effectively. If the leader is not well-liked, any attempts at communication will likely lose the desired impact. Even praise will not be positively received.

- There are seven communication strategies for Quick Wins:

   1. **Using the Power of Persuasion**
      School leaders' influence brings people within a school together and shapes the culture. This is separate from simply telling folks what to do. The idea is to provide a framework of collaboration to shape a community toward caring and mutual learning that permeates throughout the school.

   2. **Delivering Performance-Based Feedback**
      Performance feedback provides information that guides behavior in the right direction. Feedback encourages the correct behavior to happen. The goal of performance feedback is simple: Help people perform to achieve results.

   3. **Reinforcing Progress Toward Subgoals**
      Subgoals are IMPACT Goals broken down into smaller goals. Leaders can establish a Quick Win by setting frequent subgoals followed by frequent performance feedback and reinforcement. The results are instantaneous if the leader has targeted the right behaviors to reinforce.

4. **Providing Feedback to Develop Self-Efficacy**
    Self-efficacy reflects confidence in people's ability to control their motivation, behavior, and social environment. Self-efficacy is not built magically. Evidence of success is needed to build self-efficacy and collective efficacy within a school, and feedback is *essential* for building efficacy.

5. **Strengthening Relationships Through Feedback**
    Leaders can use feedback to strengthen team relationships. During turnarounds, leaders must attempt to catch people doing things right.

6. **Using Constructive Feedback for Helping People Improve**
    Doing nothing is doing something. By not correcting subpar performance, you are condoning it! Avoiding confrontation allows for subpar performance to occur and be maintained. Help, not harm. Corrective feedback should be constructive by nature to help the person perform better and should not be used as a means of confrontation or punishment. By delivering positive feedback four times more often than constructive feedback (4:1 rule), your constructive feedback will be better received and more productive, and change can be observed to occur almost immediately.

7. **Using Graphic Feedback to Strengthen Belief**
    Graphs can be shared to show more than results. They should be shared as performance feedback, highlighting collective behaviors that lead to the desired results. The ultimate goal of performance feedback is to help your staff grow in targeted skills. Graphic feedback is a simple and powerful tool for influencing behavior. Graphing progress is a very efficient and highly effective means of motivating staff.

Sustain It:

- A process for collecting, sharing, and analyzing data should be included in every leader's toolkit during a school turnaround. How might you incorporate this process into your turnaround efforts? Specifically, what behaviors will you engage in? Consider the following:

    1. Define behavior specifically: What do you want people to do?

    2. Get a baseline: Discover where the performance is.

    3. Observe and measure.

    4. Watch the performance happen and provide positive feedback. How might you share the feedback with stakeholders?

    5. Reinforce using graphic and verbal feedback until the skill is being performed at an acceptable level. How will you know when this has occurred?

CHAPTER 7:

Quick Wins:
Important Strategies and Tactics

Anyone going through a turnaround, regardless of position or tenure at the school, knows it's not easy! Leading a turnaround is equally or more challenging and depends on your ability to lead. Below are some additional strategies and tactics to consider when implementing Quick Wins.

Use the 4:1 Rule

During high uncertainty and change periods, people need more positive feedback and recognition than usual. They need confirmation that what they are doing is on target and correct. As we mentioned earlier, the 4:1 rule can be mighty powerful for building change, especially in the presence of low morale. The rule is: Give positive feedback four times as often as constructive feedback.

Target your feedback to a few specific desired behaviors that you would like to see from the person, monitor the behaviors, and if you see improvement, provide that positive feedback. If you like the behavior but there is still room for improvement, give positive feedback: "I've seen progress in the way you've been instructing the new curriculum."

Keep your feedback positive. Don't say, "I've seen great progress in how you've been doing X, *but* I think you could be even better." No buts! People will listen for the "but" whenever you give positive feedback. (We will come back to the "but" shortly.)

Regarding constructive feedback, only some people have been formally trained on how to give and receive it. So, some of us need clarification on our skills in this area. Further, providing constructive feedback during high tension is more difficult because people are more likely to react defensively.

It is important to remember that constructive feedback is necessary for improving results. People will appreciate your constructive feedback if it helps them succeed.

Always remember, the intent is to help, not hinder. If you are faced with a defensive person, first recognize that the receiver is probably under stress. That will often lead people to react more defensively than usual. It's important to stay calm and not take their reaction personally. Listen to what the person is saying, not only how he's saying it. Respond to the person's concerns sensitively and refocus the conversation on the issue at hand when appropriate.

Immediate Feedback Is Best

The more immediate the feedback, the better. When it comes to performance, the best-case scenario is to provide feedback in real-time, just as a coach would during a game. This lets you reinforce emerging behavior and allows you the opportunity to alter behavior immediately and then reinforce correct behavior as it occurs later.

While immediacy is essential, frequency of feedback is also paramount. There needs to be more than one opportunity for immediate feedback to help people learn new skills. Can you imagine a boxing coach showing a fighter how to throw a combination and then expecting them to climb into the ring and effectively perform? Of course not! Learning new skills requires frequent and immediate feedback.

While it is unrealistic to think that you can observe all performance immediately, you can create systems using your leadership team and coaches to provide frequent feedback on just a few targeted goals. You can also ask your staff questions about their performance related to some targeted skill: "How is it working?" "What did you do to make that happen?" "What will you do next time?" This type of questioning allows you to reinforce and possibly give corrective feedback (Laipple, 2012).

Avoid the "Big But" Error

Another prevalent feedback error is the "big but" error. You've heard it before, and you've probably used it recently. It goes something like: "You did a great job ... but ... ." Daniels (2016) likens the "but" to a great eraser that effectively eliminates any positive statement that was made beforehand.

Using "but" may eliminate the benefits of any positive feedback you give in the future, as the person being praised is simply waiting for the other shoe to drop—the "but." Other "big buts" come in different forms, including "however," "it's just that," "next time," and others. Avoid the "big but" error.

To do so, simply eliminate the praise and provide corrective feedback. If you've developed a good relationship using your 4:1 rule, you'll have nothing to worry about!

It's Not What You Say, It's How You Say It!

Good communication to deliver constructive feedback will help you positively influence behavior. While verbal and written communication skills are essential, researchers continue to find that both verbal and nonverbal communication is important to focus on as leaders. How can you improve your communication skills to make your feedback more effective? Here are a couple of tips to guide you.

Keep it short and sweet. You might quickly lose interest when you hear a talk or lecture that lasts way too long. You might begin looking for the quickest escape route!

Now, think about the last time you gave someone feedback—how long did you take to deliver the message? Did the person get the message?

You can immediately increase your effectiveness by providing *brief, meaningful* feedback. Brief communications are more effective when influencing behavior, especially when the goal is a correction.

We talked before about body language, and we'll revisit it here, given the large influence it can have on staff. During any interaction, especially when providing feedback, body language becomes *incredibly* important. Our bodies are much like a transmitter that is constantly pumping out signals. You must be aware of what signals you are transmitting and understand their impact on the people around you.

One time Paul's son asked, "Daddy, why do you look angry?" At that moment, he looked into the nearest mirror and realized his son was right—he *did* look angry! The problem was, he wasn't angry at all. He was just deep in thought. He will never know how often people thought he was mad when he was just thinking. Be aware of how your facial expression looks to others.

Behaviors such as crossing your arms may be perceived as defensive and knitting your brows may be perceived as being in disagreement and can quickly put your staff and students on the defensive.

When giving constructive feedback, try relaxing your body language and addressing your staff or students calmly. Some students (and adults, imagine that!) may want to upset you. You may have witnessed this occur when some couples argue or if you've ever worked with students labeled "defiant."

When these students and adults recognize even the tiniest behavioral cues that indicate you may be upset, you can be sure that they will quickly "push those buttons" to evoke your reaction the same way one would push buttons on a game controller. Each time your body language changes, even slightly, you are communicating. For whatever reason, some individuals may find an angry or irritated response gratifying. The key here is not to react but to remain calm.

Quick Wins and Emails

Unfortunately, as you have learned, many people are poor observers of their behavior and its impact on others. This includes verbal behavior, both vocal and written (e.g., emails, texts, etc.). And here's the thing: When it comes to written communication, we are missing all the data that come in the form of body language to help us to understand the communicator's intent best. As a result, emails and texts can easily be misinterpreted, creating havoc.

Even the latency between responses to emails and texts can have unintended impacts. In some cases, delayed responses can be interpreted by the sender as indicators of low engagement or disinterest in the subject or the sender. In other cases, an immediate response might signal high engagement or increased interest in the subject or perhaps "respect" for the sender. In the end, in either case, it may be that the responder was simply busy with other things or had an immediate moment to respond. The time between the email and the response had nothing to do with engagement or respect!

Not all principals are seasoned or have had a great mentor who gave them a chance to learn from their mistakes. We remember a colleague calling on us intermittently for support. He was very stressed. "Sorry, I walked to the office to find you and then to the lunchroom, but I didn't see either of you there. We need to talk!" Apparently, he had just received an email from the principal that upset him. It said, "Please come see me as soon as possible." The email, which was relatively short and to the point, left him with many questions. An important one was that he didn't know if he was in trouble for something. So before going to the principal, he wanted to know if we'd "heard" anything. We replied that we had not but empathized with him that we might have felt the same way had we received a similar email. It's not that the principal was a bad person or someone to be feared; however, she didn't necessarily instill a feeling of safety in the folks on his team. And she had sent similar emails when she was "displeased" regarding a faculty or staff member's performance. Therefore, the less clear she was in her email, the more variable the response might be given the recipient's history with her. If you've had anything in your history where a similar ambiguous statement was made as an antecedent to something terrible, it might elicit a similar response from you.

As it turned out, the principal had a birthday card for one of the other team members that she was trying to get everybody to sign before giving it to him. While the panic our colleague experienced was all for nothing, it's easy to see why he hit the panic button. And while some folks with positional authority might suggest people just "get over it," that's poor leadership and management and it comes at a cost. Beyond the emotional cost to the receiving teacher, it also came at a cost to the school at the combined rate of his time worrying about it, attempting to find us, discussing it with us, and our time listening and providing our two cents. Add to that the potential impact on morale and performance and it can have a devastating ripple effect across the school, impacting student behavior and achievement.

You see, communication isn't about the communicator's intent—it's about their impact. While her intent appeared noble, the communication receiver did not experience it this way. We've seen this act as the killer of morale and performance across many schools and organizations, as emails sent out to employees are perceived differently than was the writer's intent.

When crafting emails, especially as a school leader, you must know your audience (e.g., personal vs. professional), and you must be very aware of the tone of your email. Our experience is that very short emails tend to leave variability in terms of the writer's intent, especially when the writer and the receiver do not have a long history of interactions. On the other hand, long emails can be a problem because they might not get read entirely. Some people suggest using emojis as a means of conveying tone. One study found that younger adults aged 18–29 believe that colleagues who use emojis appear "more fun, more approachable, and kinder." The same study suggests that employees 45 and older perceive emojis as "annoying" and "unprofessional." If you notice, there is a big gap in these data regarding 30–44-year-old employees. It would be essential to know what they think!

So, what's the takeaway? Improving communication via emails can be a very powerful, Quick Win. But communication is extremely complex and can profoundly impact the listener. And because much of the "data" are missing in written communication such as emails, these forms of communication can become a challenge as there is increased variability of interpretation by the receiver(s). In the case of schools, this means faculty, staff, parents, community members, district personnel, and more. As a school leader, you need to be aware of your audience when crafting your message to increase the likelihood your communicative intent will be received as intended. In addition, avoid assuming. Instead, seek out feedback from the receivers from time to time to gauge their perception. A simple survey regarding emails can be very revealing. Questions related to frequency, length, and tone can provide essential data on the current impact of emails in your school. Whether the emails are coming from you, your team, or others, it's important to have this information. You might also ask how faculty and staff feel about emojis. Perhaps your culture will support them. Perhaps not. But why not let the data do the talking?

Quick Takeaways:

- Use the 4:1 rule to give positive feedback four times as often as constructive feedback.

- Target your feedback to a few specific desired behaviors that you would like to see from the person, monitor the behaviors, and if you see improvement, provide that positive feedback.

- Keep your feedback positive.

- Deliver feedback immediately when possible. The more immediate and frequent the feedback, the better. Learning new skills requires *frequent* and immediate feedback.

- Avoid the "big but" error.

- Keep constructive feedback short and sweet. You can immediately increase your effectiveness by providing *brief, meaningful* feedback.

- During any interaction, body language is important. Be aware of the behavioral cues you transmit and understand their impact on the people around you.

- Try relaxing your body language and addressing folks calmly when giving constructive feedback.

- When it comes to written communication, there are missing elements in the form of body language and tone of voice to help us understand the communicator's intent. Emails and texts can easily be misinterpreted, leading to unintended miscommunication.

Sustain It:

- What specific strategies can you implement to ensure you deliver feedback immediately and frequently? What might be ways to do this? Describe them.

- What alternative phrases can you use to avoid the "big but" when delivering feedback?

- What might be some ways to check on the delivery of your feedback to others? How would you solicit this feedback?

CHAPTER 8:

Quick Wins and Training for Sustainability

Quick Wins aren't just about getting things going in the right direction and keeping them going. Sometimes it means people will need to learn the skills to do what is necessary. There are many times when Quick Wins will require training. Training and learning are differentiated because learning is the intended *result* of training. And the measure of learning can be found in the behavior of the individual trained. Training is an antecedent strategy that is typically geared toward improving performance. However, it can often waste time and resources, resulting in less learning and performance.

Different variables may explain the lack of learning (Kirkpatrick & Kirkpatrick, 2007). One variable might be learner engagement. In other words, was the training provided meaningful to those attending, and did the trainer provide the information in a way that captured the learners' interest? Another variable might be knowledge gained. Even with the most engaging professional developer, the intended knowledge transference does not necessarily occur. And finally, after the training, do the learners display the behaviors required under natural working conditions that demonstrate the knowledge and skill sets provided at the training? Moreover, if they are, are they performing these behaviors fluently? In education, building fluency post-training is a process that is often left up to the teachers through an approach known as deliberate practice (Bronkhorst et al., 2014). Where regular practice typically includes mindless repetitions, deliberate practice requires purposeful attention to a precise skill or some aspect, to systematically improve performance.

Malcolm Gladwell (2011) states that "outliers" typically require at least 10,000 hours of practice for an individual to become an expert (*Outliers* is a fun book, by the way!). However, the 10,000-hour rule is a bit of a stretch as people learn at different rates. Moreover, the quality of the learning opportunity significantly impacts learning. Besides, this is a book about Quick Wins, not slow wins! While fluency often necessitates deliberate practice in education, if learners repeatedly perform a skill differently from how they were trained, they will inadvertently get good at doing something poorly.

To promote learning in any school-sponsored training, professional development, in-service, etc., there needs to be a system that provides multiple learning opportunities with built-in formative assessments to allow for continuous improvement. Formative assessment data allow you to adjust learning opportunities as needed. These often come from pre-and post-training assessments and follow-up surveys. We advocate for the use of quick performance metrics that come in the form of simply asking the individuals to perform what they just learned. Complexity is the enemy of execution and scalability, so keep it simple!

Finally, for people to use the skills they were trained in within the school setting, there needs to be a good coaching model that supports the intended learning. Training faculty and staff to be fluent in a given skill often proves difficult, if not impossible depending on the size of an initiative. And getting them actually to use the skill can be even more challenging. This is where coaching in the work environment is critical. The coaching model's goal should be to help learners move from getting a new set of skills started to helping them become habitual. This type of coaching should be precise, purposeful, and systematic. Or what is known as "deliberate coaching" (Gavoni & Weatherly, 2019), an extension of deliberate practice to the coaching process for accelerating performance improvement. According to Gavoni and Weatherly (2019), to adhere to the core principles of deliberate coaching, administrators or any professionals charged with supporting educator performance should ensure their coaching is:

Precise: Pinpointed behaviors and results are targeted and measured, with feedback that links this behavior to results.

Purposeful: Sustained focus is on a few behaviors at a time as opposed to many.

Systematic: The coaching cycle has a heavy emphasis on metrics and a steady stream of feedback to shape or reinforce incremental improvement toward a desired performance goal.

Training folks in Quick Wins and then supporting the transference of skills into the natural environment through deliberate coaching might be thought of as progressing through three phases:

1. **LAUNCHING QUICK WINS** requires implementing antecedent strategies such as planning, goal setting, and training. Essentially telling and showing faculty and staff what needs to be done to get their behavior moving in the right direction.

2. **MAKING QUICK WINS WORK** shifts from telling to asking questions such as "What did you do? What did you see as a result? What can I do to help?" and using data and feedback to shape improvement. The goal is to help educators better recognize the alignment between their behavior and the outcomes they see.

3. **Sustaining Quick Wins** involves the stakeholders in making any adjustments to the initial plan, as the data indicate. The goal is to refine processes until they become as efficient and effective as possible.

Because change tends to be hard for people, we tend to fall back on old habits. This process is geared toward getting faculty and staff to attempt a new skill or approach so that they will get in touch with some sort of positive reinforcement. Once their behavior is moving, they then have the opportunity to receive deliberate coaching. The ultimate goal is for learners of a new skill to come in contact with positive reinforcement. This should transition from the coach's positive feedback and fade to the natural reinforcement (success!) available for implementing the new skills as intended. When faculty and staff see or experience the benefits of the skill, they move from "having to do it" to "wanting to do it."

For example, because Principal Daniels asked faculty and staff what changes they wanted at Hawkins Heights, they were willing to try the new initiatives. As such, they began engaging in behaviors such as showing up to their posts, greeting students, asking them to walk back if they ran, etc. It wasn't long before they directly experienced the positive outcome associated with their behavior in the form of students following expectations, reduced disruptions, and a general sense of improved well-being. When faculty and staff began experiencing these positive outcomes, they didn't need to be told to be at their posts. They were happy to be there. Eventually, their behavior became a habit, and their collective behavior became part of the culture or "the way we do things here." It is under these conditions that change initiatives become sustainable.

Making Training and Coaching Work

When engaging in Quick Wins and change initiatives, use principles of institutionalization to increase the likelihood that stakeholders will be engaged and habits will stick. This simply means involving the group in designing and implementing the action plan as a Quick Wins intervention. According to Sigurdsson and Austin (2006), this can be accomplished by:

- Training and involving educators in developing an action plan
- Training educators in the implementation of the action plan
- Involving educators in collecting data on performance measures and reporting out
- Involving educators in the dispensing of consequences (e.g., positive feedback, corrective feedback)

Institutionalization can be thought of as a Quick Win for culture change and sustainability. Quick Wins become part of the culture as everybody is involved in the process. The old saying goes, "If they author it, they'll own it." As you've learned, involving people in targeting and developing Quick Win initiatives drastically increases the likelihood the Quick Wins will happen.

Leveraging Positive Reinforcement

Ultimately, if you want initiatives to stick, you have to leverage the most powerful tool in your toolbox for bringing out the best in people: positive reinforcement.

Remember we talked earlier about using accomplishments to accelerate the achievement of Quick Wins. Suppose you want training or any change initiative to stick. In that case, you must provide faculty and staff with regular recognition and rewards (find out what is meaningful to them!) to deliver positive reinforcement for achieving accomplishments and subgoals. If you remember, accomplishments might be measured by the number of tasks that have occurred associated with their responsibilities and duties including: the completion of a plan; the number of people who have been trained; the number of staff members observed; the number of staff members receiving feedback related to the training; the number of times data were collected and reported out, etc.

Measuring Positive Relationships

Accomplishments can also be measured by the number of positive relationships developed over time, which is often a function of school leadership. These can easily be measured through direct observations of people greeting each other in the hallway, positive interactions between staff, students, and leadership, and the number of faculty volunteering for extra duties. Climate and culture survey data let you and your leadership team know that things are moving in the right direction. They also put you in a position to deliver positive reinforcement to your leadership team. By the way, accomplishing goals in and of themselves often serves as positive reinforcement if the goals you've collaboratively determined are rooted in shared values. In other words, they are IMPACT Goals.

Reinforcing Subgoals

Recognizing subgoals on the way to achieving goals is just a way to put you in the position of delivering more positive reinforcement to faculty and staff for their hard work. And as we mentioned, if truly value-driven goals have been established with faculty and staff, this creates a true "win-win" situation for the school's stakeholders. Remember, using strategies involving positive reinforcement is the only way to get "want to do" behavior, as opposed to using strategies based on negative reinforcement (fear of consequences) that create "have to do" behavior.

While both methods get behavior change, only positive reinforcement results in a strong learning culture characterized by people going above and beyond.

We've seen the proof: The frequency of behavior issues in schools that use these approaches drop drastically while student achievement and teacher retention increase dramatically. Such is the power of behavior-specific positive reinforcement.

Quick Takeaways:

- Quick Wins aren't just about getting things going in the right direction: They are about sustaining them.

- Training and learning are differentiated because learning is the intended *result* of training. And the measure of learning can be found in the behavior of the individual trained.

- Training is an antecedent strategy geared toward improving performance.

- For people to use the skills they were trained in, there needs to be a good coaching model that supports the intended learning.

- The coaching model's goal should be to help learners move from getting a new set of skills to helping them develop habits and to support the transference of skills into the natural environment.

- Using principles of institutionalization, involve the group in designing and implementing the action plan as an intervention.

- Leverage using positive reinforcement if you want initiatives to stick.

- Use accomplishments to accelerate the achievement of Quick Wins. Provide faculty and staff with regular recognition and rewards for accomplishments and subgoals.

- Using strategies involving positive reinforcement is the only way to get "want to do" behavior, as opposed to using strategies based on negative reinforcement (fear of consequences) that create "have to do" behavior.

Sustain It:

- How would you determine if faculty and staff required training on Quick Win initiatives?

- As a leader-coach, what behaviors would you need to engage in to help your faculty and staff become better performers by extending learning opportunities into the school and classroom environment?

- What systems need to be considered to implement an effective coaching model? Assess what you already have in place and what updates and modifications may be needed to make the system run effectively and efficiently. Consider making your coaching process deliberate.

QUICK WINS
IN ACTION

CHAPTER 9:

Improving Behavior in the Cafeteria

Earlier, we introduced the Quick Win Matrix to assist you with identifying and evaluating potential Quick Wins. Specifically, we suggested that you identify Quick Wins based on:

- The impact the Quick Win will bring to the school.

- The visibility the Quick Win has to everyone watching the school's turnaround.

- The effort to implement the Quick Win is easily achievable using the school's and district's resources.

This chapter is dedicated to providing you with a story of how Quick Wins are effectively applied in the cafeteria. The goal is to bring the principles outlined in *Quick Wins* to life through detailed and sometimes humorous real-life examples and experiences. We've chosen to provide extensive details in this chapter as many of the strategies outlined are generalizable to almost any common area (for example, the hallways during arrival and dismissal). Moreover, there seems to be a scarcity of information on this topic, and schools, especially those mired with behavioral challenges, typically struggle in this area.

Conquering the Cafeteria

Suppose you have worked at a school where misbehavior is common. In that case, there is a good chance that you dread visiting the cafeteria during student lunch or frequently experience dismay at the Pandora's box of behavior resulting from poorly managed cafeterias during the latter part of the school day. Make no mistake, over-stimulation in the cafeteria has the potential to affect every student and staff member negatively. This inevitably will impact student achievement. This is a significant reason Principal Daniels and the team decided to focus on the cafeteria as one of their initial Quick Wins.

Student lunch is a good place where an observer might take the "temperature" of the school. Negative climate (shared perceptions) and culture (shared behaviors) can slowly creep down hallways, into the front office, and eventually into the classroom. If that sounds like an ad for a horror flick, then we have the same vision.

The Silent Lunch Fallacy

While in the cafeteria under less-structured conditions, one might observe some well-meaning staff march to the front of the cafeteria, pick up the microphone as if it were a weapon, and then forcibly declare, "That's it! SILENT LUNCH!" Principal Daniels observed this as he walked through the cafeteria when he visited the school the year before. Every time we see this, we yell, "Sir, please put the microphone down and step away … slowly." We've seen this play out many times across many schools, especially elementary schools. The funny thing is it never works!

We are not sure what happens to folks when they enter the cafeteria. Most of them are great people who typically behave benevolently—at least outside of the cafeteria! However, once they cross the threshold that separates the cafeteria from the rest of the world, they enter a parallel dimension: one where an alternative self who prefers reprimand to reinforcement takes over. Think of it as *Invasion of the Body Snatchers* or a never-ending episode of *Breaking Bad*!

In one cafeteria, we experienced a bit of a *Twilight Zone* after observing countless reprimands of students by staff. Then we observed a monitor whom we caught smiling and praising a couple of students. We were busy with a student, so we asked a colleague to let her know that we recognized and appreciated her positive interactions with the students. To our chagrin, she began to cry! Can you believe that? Cry! Talk about a parallel universe.

But think about this: Suppose you are part of a cafeteria culture slowly drifting to the dark side. In that case, your efforts at positive interaction with students might be perceived as a weakness or even anti-administration. That is precisely what she later expressed to us. She also mentioned it was "so nice to hear positive feedback." Apparently, she (as were the students) was positive feedback-deprived … further evidence of a negative culture.

After witnessing similar scenes play out across other schools, we decided we needed to intervene. Like any good behaviorist, we began collecting data on student and staff behavior variables. Because the "silent lunch" demands were ineffective (actually doing more harm than good) and appeared to be random, we decided it might be helpful to collect data on the decibel levels in the cafeteria that evoked the "silent lunch" command from staff.

We found no evident pattern regarding the decibel level that prompted staff to initiate the punishment. Decibel levels were all over the place. The reason students were placed on silent lunch appeared to be primarily based on the attending staff's cultural norms, mood, perception, and noise tolerance.

So, we collected data on time—specifically, how long it took for students to begin talking again after the staff declared "silent lunch." Any guesses? Almost reliably, between 45 and 60 seconds later, a few students would begin whispering, and then a few more, and pretty soon, the whole cafeteria was chatting away. The result ... just hit replay. The same staff said the same thing and got the same results. We thought we were into *Groundhog Day* territory now. Fortunately, we were armed with the science of behavior to break the cycle.

The staff was getting caught up in what classroom management guru Glenn Latham (1998) called a criticism trap, whereby the tendency is to "catch students behaving bad" as opposed to recognizing their "good" or improved behavior. Perhaps they had not been trained and coached to fluency in basic procedures for managing behavior. There might be rules on the wall and possibly "training" generally related to behavior. Still, there is no way they would continue to use ineffective strategies such as "silent lunch" if they knew better.

Something needed to happen, and that something required a team approach.

The Secret Sauce: Teamwork

As leaders, behavior analysts, and coaches who have successfully turned around failing schools, we can tell you that improving the behavior in any common area within the school requires teamwork. "There is no 'I' in team" fits the cafeteria, as no one person can fix it.

We've often walked into a cafeteria, and an administrator or staff member has said, "Thank goodness you are here! Can you get these kids to behave?" The answer is "No, we can't!" At least we can't do it sustainably. Much like the staff member who grabs the mic and demands a silent lunch, anything we do solo will only result in a temporary fix. We love coach John Wooden's story on the importance of teamwork, where he notes that, despite being stacked with superstars such as Kobe Bryant, Karl Malone, and Shaquille O'Neal, the 2004 USA Olympic Basketball team failed to win a gold medal. The reason, as Wooden notes: is that the USA sent great *players*, while the countries who won the gold and silver medals sent great *teams*.

Unless you have a very small cafeteria, managing cafeteria behavior in schools that struggle with misbehavior is simply too much for one person, even a superstar. While the person who continually grabs the mic to demand silent lunch may be practicing fruitless behavior, it's been our experience that they often do their best to carry the ball by themselves, despite being surrounded by a team. In their mind, they are taking action while the rest of the cafeteria team sits on their hands. It's not that the rest of the team is lazy or weak. They are more likely to not possess the self-efficacy for managing student behavior due to limited mastery experiences. In other words, if they have not seen their efforts work in the past, they likely do not believe in their ability to manage behavior.

And let's not forget the armchair quarterbacking that occurs from some administrators or staff regularly in the cafeteria. It's easy to say, "Do this, do that," but managing the cafeteria requires more than talk. It demands a systematic and consistent approach from those on the front line, from the teacher who leads students to the cafeteria, and from administrators who structure and support all efforts. What follows is a detailed approach to improving the cafeteria as a Quick Win that we applied across different school settings. While your cafeteria might look different, most strategies outlined can apply to any large-scale change.

Staff Performance in the Cafeteria

Nobody wants to waste time consistently managing chronic misbehavior. We believe that administrators, teachers, and support staff desire to perform well, for students to achieve, and for misbehavior to remain at a minimum. School employees at all levels need to be taught better (not told). First, let's take a look at some principles that might seem simple but are fundamental to a successful Quick Win in a cafeteria where behavior is challenging. Then we will behaviorally unpack them.

- **ESTABLISH STAFF EXPECTATIONS.** Staff should know precisely what to do, how to do it, where to stand and walk, what they should monitor, and what they should say and do under specific conditions (more on this later). Also, they should know what they should do when students are behaving well, and how to correct misbehavior.

- **BE CONSISTENT.** Consistency is key. If staff fail to reinforce desirable behavior, you are unlikely to see improvement in behavior. If staff fail to correct misbehavior effectively, you will almost definitely see more problem behaviors because the perception will be that the misbehavior is being condoned.

- **CREATE VISIBLE IMPACT.** The positive impact of staff performance must be visible to them. If not, there is a good chance staff will stop performing or will perform only when you are present and watching.

These principles might seem like common sense, but the behaviors associated with them tend to be uncommon in cafeterias where behavior is challenging. So, let's look at what some of those behaviors should look like.

When students behave well (following rules and expectations), staff should:

- **PROVIDE NONCONTINGENT ATTENTION TO STRENGTHEN DESIRABLE BEHAVIOR.** For example, sincerely asking students about their week-end, how school is going, or if they watched the latest game. This is termed "noncontingent" attention but is contingent on rule-following behavior. In other words, don't initiate conversation when a student is out of his assigned area or yelling out across the cafeteria. This might inadvertently encourage more misbehavior! The point of noncontingent attention is that it provides students with positive attention for desirable behaviors.

- **PRAISE THE SPECIFIC BEHAVIOR YOU WANT TO SEE.** While some folks use the microphone only for correcting misbehavior, we recommend the opposite. Try to use the mic to reinforce improvements in behavior. The same person who picks up the mic 5 minutes into lunch after students begin screaming across to other tables might use it 4 minutes into lunch to recognize and thank students for being "responsible" by speaking with only the students at their table. The time interval here can be progressively increased. (By the way, don't waste your breath if the praise isn't sincere. Nobody wants praise if they don't believe the person delivering it means it. To us, it is worse than being reprimanded!)

When students misbehave, it is staffs' job to correct misbehavior:

- **CONSISTENTLY.** This means *do not ignore* misbehavior. We hear seasoned educators recommend "ignoring" all the time as a behavioral intervention. We want to be a little more precise in its use. From our perspective, "planned ignoring" is great when students who *desire* your attention misbehave to obtain your attention. But ignoring students misbehaving and not wanting your attention is an instant failure. If staff does not consistently correct misbehavior, it spreads like wildfire. It also subverts staff who are consistently attempting to correct misbehavior.

- **RESPECTFULLY.** Always treat students with dignity and respect—of course—but this does not mean you should not correct misbehavior. It means avoiding sarcastic and condescending tones and consistently correcting misbehavior in a businesslike manner. It also means sticking to the 4:1 rule. If you correct misbehavior, make it a point to return to that student in the future with four more positive interactions, as illustrated above. Remember, you are trying to create a cafeteria culture for everyone to enjoy.

Teacher Behavior

Are you thinking, "But teachers aren't in the cafeteria, so why is this part of their responsibility?" If you suspect teachers feel this way, you may want to explain how common areas have a major impact throughout the school that pushes into their classroom, like a running back driving for a first down. Help them understand that being a team player in this area will positively impact their class and the school campus. Also, tell them not to worry as their part is relatively easy.

- **TEACHERS SHOULD TEACH CAFETERIA RULES AND EXPECTATIONS IN THE FIRST DAYS OF SCHOOL.** Use a map of the cafeteria to explain the transition routine and behavioral expectations.

- **TEACHERS SHOULD REMIND STUDENTS OF THESE EXPECTATIONS BEFORE THE STUDENTS TRANSITION INTO THE CAFETERIA.** In a relay race, it is the responsibility of the baton holder to transition the baton smoothly to the next runner to maintain continuity and velocity in a race. Reminding students of the expectations is called pre-correcting. By reminding students of the expectations of the cafeteria, the teacher is setting up a smooth transition for the students and the cafeteria monitor.

Reclaiming the Cafeteria: The Plan

Now, the above principles and critical behaviors are critical to success but getting faculty, staff, and students to engage in them is where the proverbial rubber meets the road. Creating engagement requires practical processes that should be driven by an easy-to-understand plan. Many of the processes covered here are areas where we strongly believe most schools fail. This has to do with the actual development of the plan, training staff to fluency in reinforcing and correcting behavior, and observing and helping these folks perform to their best ability. Remember, staff in the cafeteria must know precisely what to do and believe they can do it to positively impact students' cafeteria behavior. Folks involved in this part of the plan should think about themselves as coaches seeking to bring out the best in their team. Here are key components and behaviors that should be a part of your cafeteria plan:

DEVELOP A MAP: To make things easy, create a cafeteria map and a simple plan that include the following:

TRAFFIC FLOW: Attempt to have students enter in one direction and leave in another. Keeping traffic moving in a single direction is a simple fix for many problems. Simply add arrows indicating student movement patterns.

STAFF POSTS: Write the staff's name in the desired location. If you know there are "hot" areas, try placing your most skilled staff in those areas. As staff becomes more skilled, you can rotate these areas weekly, monthly, or quarterly to avoid burnout.

AREAS STAFF SHOULD MONITOR: While the staff is collectively responsible for supporting appropriate behavior across the cafeteria, having an assigned area to monitor allows for more focused observations.

EXPECTATIONS REGARDING STAFF BEHAVIOR: These should be specific, such as where they should walk as they monitor and what they should say and do, as outlined earlier.

BEHAVIOR STAFF WILL FOCUS ON REINFORCING: We wrote earlier about how staff can reinforce through noncontingent attention and specific praise. Try to match praise with what is desirable to the students. We divide praise into four types:

1.   **QUIET PRAISE:** This is good to use with older students or those who dislike receiving praise in public. Examples of quiet praise are a subtle thumbs up, a well-timed nod of the head, or a simple smile following a desirable behavior.

2.   **INDIVIDUAL PRAISE:** This is simply providing praise to an individual displaying a desirable behavior (remember to be behavior-specific). Be careful not to fall into the trap of correcting misbehavior and only praising the appropriate behavior once the student displays it. If you need to praise a student for following the directive (following redirection may be a "new" behavior for some students), try to differentiate this praise from the praise you typically provide. For example, make praise less enthusiastic, or minimize your eye contact.

3.   **GROUP PRAISE:** This is just like it sounds. You might praise a group of students for doing well or for showing improvement: "The students at table 2 are on point today with their conversation levels!"

4.   **PIVOT PRAISE:** This involves praising a student behaving as expected as a prompt to a nearby student who is not. When the nearby student begins following the expectation, the staff then "pivots" to that student and praises them. Like the planned ignoring strategy discussed earlier, this tactic is typically best for students who desire your attention. Implement this strategy to avoid giving an off-task or misbehaving student desirable attention for undesirable behavior.

RULES AND EXPECTATIONS REGARDING STUDENT BEHAVIOR: Teach students appropriate behaviors that are incompatible with misbehavior. In the cafeteria, common problem behaviors are students talking loudly and leaving their assigned area. Train staff on the strategies above to reinforce appropriate cafeteria behavior. Consider embedding the following in your rules and expectations:

•   Students face forward with their feet on the ground.

•   Students request permission to leave their seat.

•   Students speak only to peers directly next to or in front of them.

DEVELOP A MENU OF CORRECTIVE CONSEQUENCES: Develop a simple menu of consequences aligned with the magnitude of misbehaviors common to the cafeteria. For example, a consequence for running in the cafeteria might be to walk back; a consequence for yelling across tables might be a brief time-out. Remember, avoid "silent lunch" as the go-to behavior management tool. If you must incorporate silent lunch as part of your plan, make sure it is not a marathon. Brief is best, like most time-outs. Essentially silent lunch is a timeout away from social reinforcement. Try 1–2 minutes, with the expectation that all students follow that expectation. If a student from the silent lunch table group talks, simply remind all students of the expectation and reset the time for 1 minute. Time-outs can be applied at the individual and small group levels.

Time-outs that are too long result in students learning they do not need to follow the expectation, as staff typically do not have the resources to ensure students maintain the time-out as expected for the designated time. For individual time-outs, 3–5 minutes works well. If you find only a few students from the group are not following the expectations of a whole group time-out, individualize their time-outs and avoid punishing the entire group.

GETTING STAFF TO BELIEVE THEY CAN DO IT: Remember that Albert Bandura's research (1986) demonstrated that self-efficacy—or belief in one's ability to accomplish a task—is one of the biggest success predictors. Remember that developing self-efficacy doesn't require hypnosis or special psychological strategies. It does require deliberately structuring conditions that allow staff to receive training in the concept and purpose of the plan and then providing ample opportunity for staff to practice (with feedback) the skills required to implement the plan.

We recommend practicing in the cafeteria. Require staff to stand, walk, and monitor the area designated in the plan. Create real-life scenarios (we're sure you have plenty) and practice staff responses. These scenarios should include staff responses that reinforce desired student behavior and strengthen relationships and responses intended to correct misbehavior. The goal is to provide as many scenarios and practice opportunities as are needed to encourage staff to respond without correction from the coach. Once staff can apply these strategies quickly and independently of feedback, they should have enough tools to get them through the initial days back from break—a small window when student misbehavior is typically low.

GETTING STAFF TO BELIEVE THEY CAN POSITIVELY IMPACT BEHAVIOR: While it is important for staff to have the requisite knowledge and skills to change cafeteria behavior, they must also believe that they can do it on game day and will achieve winning results. If you remember, belief in one's ability to produce an outcome is called response efficacy.

Suppose we spend months demonstrating to staff effective techniques for flying. We practice flapping our arms and getting a running start. The staff becomes proficient in the flying procedures and flawlessly demonstrates them under practice conditions. We have very high self-efficacy in flapping our arms and running. But on the big day, we are lined up atop the cliff ready for launch ... and there is a 100% chance that no one will jump. The reason is obvious: They do not truly believe they can fly! In short, they have no response efficacy.

Our point is that if staff implements procedures after training without our prodding them, they must believe that they can do it and that a positive outcome will result. This is the driving force behind what is commonly known as grit. You won't see grit if folks do not believe their efforts will bear fruit. However, if they believe they can do it, believe it will achieve the expected outcome, and value it, they will push through adversity to reach the goal.

Deliberate Coaching

As part of your cafeteria plan, leaders must help launch and secure designees to support and coach the initial implementation. Having a vision, a plan that outlines precise expectations, and training is a great start, but it is insufficient for success. While staff may have been trained to some level of fluency, they will tend to fall back on their old habits. Remember that administrators and designees should act like coaches, purposefully and systematically helping their team perform well enough to be successful.

While these "coaches" can model once or twice how to perform a specific skill under actual live cafeteria conditions, they must refrain from praising and correcting student misbehavior by themselves. Instead, they should be focused on prompting the cafeteria staff to do it. At this point, staff should know what to do. Getting the staff to engage in the expected behaviors is important for building self-efficacy and helping the staff develop instructional control. It is important that students view all adults in the cafeteria as having authority, not just the administrators and others tasked with "coaching" the cafeteria. Instructional control will naturally develop through consistent reinforcement and correction applied by each staff member.

For example, rather than asking a student to sit facing forward, the coach should point out the student to cafeteria staff, ask them what they might do to correct the behavior, and then prompt them to do it while the coach observes. If the monitor has already asked the student to sit facing forward and the student is again turned around yelling at another table, an effective coach might ask what the staff will do next. Remember, their responses to expected and challenging behavior should have already been laid out in the cafeteria plan and taught to them. Asking allows the coach to reinforce correct responses or assess and provide guidance for incorrect responses.

If the staff responds incorrectly, the coach might use simple questioning strategies to enhance critical thinking skills rather than telling them what they should do. For example, "Remember, you've already redirected the student on what to do. You've even given pivot praise to students in the area who were on task. What's next on the hierarchy of responses for continued misbehavior?" Then, suppose they are still unable to come up with the correct response. In that case, the coach might say, "As you've already redirected and used pivot praise, you should now provide a warning by first stating the consequences for following expectations and then the consequences for continued misbehavior." Then the coach might ask the staff to role-play how to deliver a warning and do it quickly. For example, "Billy, I've asked you once to sit facing forward and speak to the students at your table. If you do, you can remain seated here. If you don't, I will require you to sit in the time-out section against the wall for 5 minutes." Again, these responses should be pre-planned, part of your cafeteria plan, and taught and practiced by staff.

Once the cafeteria folks are performing adequately, it is up to the coach to help them see the positive impact of their collective efforts. At this point, the measures we discussed will become your best friend, like a coach referring to the scoreboard who says, "Look, team, the plays you are running are working. We are winning!"

Staff will begin believing in themselves and their collective effort when measures are pumped back that demonstrate the improved student behavior that has resulted from their individual and collective behavior. Sometimes improvement is hard to see because staff suffering from confirmation bias (the tendency to notice what confirms their existing beliefs) may focus only on the negative, such as, "We knew these kids wouldn't behave." They may still see a few students yelling across tables and believe things are the same as ever. But data indicating a 50% reduction of out-of-seat behavior, for example, are almost certain to have a positive influence and strengthen belief in the system as well as the collective efficacy of the team.

Remember the concept of leading and lagging indicators we discussed in an earlier chapter? Well, leading indicators should be used to reinforce staff performance and are most effective when used immediately in the beginning, then faded to daily and weekly use. For example, the number of students in a time-out section can be used as a leading indicator. As the number reduces, the coach can use the data to make progress visible and thus reinforce staff behavior as they can begin "seeing" a valued outcome. Even if it's only initially in the form of a data point.

Use lagging indicators weekly and monthly as an ongoing measure of results. A short email to the team and the school from the principal might say something along the lines of, "As a result of the collective efforts of the cafeteria staff, teachers, and coaches with following the plan, we've had a 37% reduction in cafeteria and afternoon referrals this week. Well done!" The frequency of this email can then be faded. If the cafeteria has historically been an issue, we recommend that data be monitored no less than monthly, even when things are going well. It doesn't take much for the culture of the cafeteria to shift. Monitoring the data is a good way to problem solve and head off potential problems that tend to become progressively more challenging. Using these strategies will also strengthen belief in the administrator or designee who has led the cafeteria-change effort. A quick and sustainable win indeed.

A Note on Cafeteria Noise

If you are disappointed that we did not focus more on "noise level" in the cafeteria, we believe that students should be able to talk normally and not in a "whisper-like" voice. The cafeteria is a time for socialization. We believe lunchtime is recharge time for students, not for staff.

However, if you feel that noise level is a problem in your cafeteria, here is what we recommend: Purchase a decibel reader. There is a variety of decibel readers available. One that we found very useful was attached to a traffic light. It remained green until the noise level moved beyond a preset point. When this happened, the light would emit a sound and turn yellow. The light would move to red if the noise level did not return to the predetermined level within a few seconds.

In one school we supported, when the light went red, students were required to remain silent for 1 minute or until the light returned to green. And when the light remained green for 15-minute intervals, the grade groups in the cafeteria would receive "stars" that would eventually allow them access to group reinforcers such as music played in the cafeteria, temporarily changing seats, or even an ice cream day.

Without some measure with feedback, it is improbable that students will be able "check" their voice levels; moreover, the staff is more likely to correct noise levels based on their mood or perception, which is often inaccurate.

Like anything else, this is just a tool. Without the processes outlined in this book, we don't know any tool that will consistently work. Case in point: We observed the same traffic light used at another school. In that school, the students would take great joy in speaking louder to get the light to change colors. The staff response to this was to readjust the decibel meter so the students could not trigger it, even if they were yelling—an excellent example of students shaping staff's behavior!

Strategic Action Planning With the End in Mind

We hope you have found this approach to managing cafeteria behavior helpful. Remember, the strategies in this section can and should be applied to any of your common areas or to any desired large-scale change. We've seen great school improvement plans that garnered poor results because the established procedures weren't followed. Educators and staff need to believe the plan is workable and that they can implement it. As discussed earlier, strategic planning with the end in mind is a robust process for ensuring your Quick Wins will be successful. In the case of the cafeteria, involving stakeholders in determining:

1. What result will serve as a measure of success (e.g., increased on-task behavior, decreased time-outs, reduced referrals)?

2. What are the expectations for students to achieve this result?

3. How will staff teach, reinforce, and correct the behaviors associated with the cafeteria expectations?

4. How will staff be trained and coached?

Strategic planning with the end in mind is a practical and systematic approach for producing quick and sustainable wins by aligning the actions of everyone who directly or indirectly impacts student behavior in the cafeteria.

Quick Takeaways:

- The cafeteria is a good place where an observer might take the "temperature" of the school.

- Improving the behavior in any common area within the school requires teamwork.

- Strategic action planning with the end in mind requires determining which results are impacted, the student and staff behaviors that will move these measures, and delivering feedback to reinforce or adjust the plan.

- To improve staff performance in the cafeteria and other common areas:

    ○ **ESTABLISH STAFF EXPECTATIONS.** Staff should know precisely what to do, how to do it, where to stand and walk, what they should monitor, and exactly what they should say and do under specific conditions. Also, they should know what they should do when students are behaving well, and how to correct misbehavior.

    ○ **BE CONSISTENT.** Being consistent is key. If staff fail to reinforce desirable behavior, you are unlikely to see improvement in behavior. If staff fail to correct misbehavior effectively, you will almost definitely see more problem behaviors because the perception will be that the misbehavior is being condoned.

    ○ **CREATE VISIBLE IMPACT.** The positive impact of staff performance must be visible to them. If not, there is a good chance staff will stop performing or perform only when you are present and watching.

- When students behave well, provide noncontingent attention to strengthen desirable behavior.

- Praise the specific behavior you want to see.

- When students misbehave, staff should correct misbehavior consistently and respectfully.

- Teacher behavior plays an important role in student behavior in common areas of the school. When a teacher reminds the students of the expectation, they set up their class for success.

Sustain It:

- Assess for Quick Wins. It's a good idea to review your current plans, processes, and systems for your school's common areas.

- Consider assessing your school's cafeteria plan. Are there some potential Quick Wins? After a QuickWOC assessment, determine if the plan needs to be updated.

- Use strategic planning with the end in mind to ensure aligned actions with key results.

CHAPTER 10:

Improving Behavior in the Classroom

Improving learner behavior in a sustainable way requires creating an environment that brings out the best in them. As a school leader, you are keenly aware that the adults in the classroom and school are a critical part of the learner's environment. Whether working with a learner, assistant, teacher, or administrator, the people you work with will want to see a meaningful difference due to your support. This difference needs to be measurable. When you help the adults in the learner's environment behave differently, and that change results in an observable improvement in the learner's or in multiple learners' behavior, the behavioral improvement often serves as a naturally occurring reinforcer. When this intervention requires low effort and produces visible and valued outcomes, the improvement is paired with your support. This reinforcement increases the likelihood the adults will buy into your leadership and plan. And when you have buy-in, others will be willing to take on greater challenges in the future. This is what's at the heart of Quick Wins. You must remember that, in a sense, the faculty and staff are learners, too.

Remember, people tend to be poor observers of their own behavior, the impact of their behavior on the environment, and the impact of the environment on their behavior. This is why using measurement to align pinpointed results with pinpointed behavior is a strategic approach to Quick Wins. In other words, make the impact of faculty and staff behaviors salient through the use of data. Now, in this case of classroom management, the pinpointed results include:

- Individual student or classroom behavior, including:
  - On-task behavior
  - Disruptive behavior
- Pinpointed teacher behaviors, including:
  - Delivering behavior-specific praise

   °   Consistently correcting misbehavior

   °   Asking lots of questions to engage students using a variety of approaches including whiteboards, response cards, choral responding, cooperative learning strategies, etc.

   °   Linking questions to academic standards

The classroom is like a small organization, complete with the teacher as the leader. The systems, processes, tasks, and behaviors are all aimed at producing an extremely important "business result." In this case, student achievement. To achieve this result, the classroom leader (teacher) should constantly assess and adjust their approach to improve their students' individual and collective performance. As a school leader, when teachers are struggling, you must put in place a practical but systematic approach to supporting them. Depending on the size of your school and the resources, you may have instructional coaches, behavioral coaches, or designees whose responsibility is to support teachers in any given area. This responsibility might fall to the assistant principal in smaller schools with fewer resources. In many cases, this is a shared responsibility involving the school leader. But whatever the case, the process should be non-evaluative and should entail gathering baseline data, engaging faculty in goal setting, planning interventions, and then using feedback to shape progress systematically.

A variety of tools allows you to collect data related to the ecology of the classroom. These data can be focused on critical pinpoints such as "positive" interactions. As you know, a staple of good leadership, including classroom leadership, is the delivery of positive reinforcement. The more the adults in the classroom provide attention to the learners when they are doing the right thing, the more likely they are to engage in that behavior, especially when they are provided behavior-specific praise and the adults have established themselves as reinforcers. And when this "right thing" aligns with critical results (e.g., reduced disruptions, increased on-task behavior, increased student achievement), magic happens.

It's been our experience that educators (well, most people, for that matter) are likely to get more of the behavior they pay the greatest attention to. Unfortunately, misbehavior often gets recognized more than appropriate behavior, even when there is a ton of appropriate behavior to recognize! Remember, the rule of thumb is 4:1. We've even heard 8:1 and a few other ratios. But, in all cases, it's a lot more positive than negative.

But how can we operationalize a positive-versus-negative interaction to collect data and further support the teacher? To do this, we must take judgment out of the equation. Positive and negative should have nothing to do with the perceived quality of the interaction between the teacher or adult and the student. It should be about what the student was doing during the interaction. If the student was engaged in appropriate behavior when the teacher responded to a student, that can be marked as a positive. If the student was engaged in inappropriate behavior and the teacher responds to the student, that is marked as a negative interaction. Judging an interaction as "good or bad" can get confusing and leave room for error. For example, if a teacher was treating a student kindly but at a time the student was off task, this would be recorded as a negative interaction. *It's about what the teacher is responding to.* And of course, these data can be coded in various ways, such as using a "B" if behavior-specific praise was used or perhaps an "R" if a reprimand was given.

Keep in mind the purpose of collecting data is not to show the teacher whether or not they are measuring up. Instead, it is to identify strengths and targeted behaviors that, if shaped, will result in a measurable decrease in disruptions and an increase in on-task behaviors. As such, the teacher should be involved in the process, and the data should be used as a measurement and feedback tool to reinforce the teacher's pinpointed behaviors. Too often, data have been used to punish; you must establish yourself as a reinforcer and earn the teachers' trust before collecting data on their behavior. They should feel confident that your observations have nothing to do with their performance evaluations and that the data collected will remain confidential. Moreover, they need to know that the data will be used to craft an appropriate intervention that improves outcomes for both the learner and teachers.

Some teachers can be resistant when it comes to behavior-related issues. And that's understandable, as behavior issues can tax a teacher's last nerve! We've heard school leaders and others in supporting roles say things like, "They'll never change. There's nothing I can do." When a teacher is resistant, they are less willing to shower students with support. But consider this: If a learner was resistant; if there was no improvement, would we say, "They'll never change. There's nothing any of us can do."? Of course not. The teacher is a learner, and you are there to bring out the best in them so they can bring out the best in their students. Suppose they aren't performing well in behavior or classroom management. The issue is related either to a skill or motivational deficit, which can be determined using the Performance Diagnostic Checklist outlined earlier.

You might have read this and been thinking, "Where is the Quick Win? Changing classroom behavior is a big task requiring lots of effort." Well, if you are thinking that, you are correct. But there are typically many Quick Wins if you know where to look. Here is a list of areas to assess for a Quick Win:

- How are students transitioning into the class in the morning?
  - Are there desks assigned?
  - Is there a bell ringer?
  - Do the students have tasks to work on when the teacher takes attendance?
- Does the teacher have an effective attention signal?
  - Does the teacher have verbal and physical prompts such as putting his or her hand up in the air?

- ° Does the teacher wait until all students stop, look, and listen before providing instruction?
- ° Do students respond within 3 seconds?
- How are the students transitioning out of the classroom?
  - ° Is there a systematic approach for lining up?
  - ° Do students do so efficiently?
- Does the teacher differentiate opportunities to respond?
  - ° Does the teacher ask an academic question before calling on a student or students?
  - ° Does the teacher use some sort of random picker when calling on students?
  - ° Does the teacher use choral responding?
  - ° Does the teacher use response cards?
  - ° Does the teacher use whiteboards?
  - ° Does the teacher use cooperative learning strategies such as turn and talk?
- Does the teacher have simple routines and expectations for common behaviors including asking for help, handing in papers, getting materials, and using the bathroom?

Now, suppose there are baseline data collected on student behavior before and after implementing the Quick Win. In that case, there is a good chance the data will do the talking in demonstrating improvement. But even without data, many of these Quick Wins will produce immediate and visible changes that the teacher can directly observe. In the end, these Quick Wins are a great way of getting the teacher's buy-in to continue improving.

Quick Takeaways:

- When you help the adults in the learner's environment behave differently, and that change results in an observable improvement in the learner's or multiple learners' behavior, the behavioral improvement often serves as a naturally occurring reinforcer.
- When you have buy-in from your stakeholders, they will be willing to take on greater challenges in the future. This is the heart of Quick Wins.

- The classroom is like a small organization, with the teacher as the leader. The systems, processes, tasks, and behaviors aim to produce a significant "business result" or student achievement.

- Some teachers can be resistant when it comes to behavior-related issues.

- The teacher is a learner, and you are there to bring out the best in them so they can bring out the best in their students.

- Changing classroom behavior is a big task requiring lots of effort. There are many Quick Wins when changing classroom behavior.

Sustain It:

- How might you evaluate teachers' classroom management systems?

- How does classroom management impact student achievement?

- What tools could you use to assess effective classroom management?

CHAPTER 11:

Customer Service and Curbside Appeal

It is common knowledge that the first interaction people have when they enter your school is with the staff in the front office. This position can be very powerful as it frequently represents the "face" of the school. Positive interactions with the front office staff serve to strengthen relationships with the community. One positive interaction can connect a missing link; however, one negative interaction can break the chain. As such, it is essential to remember it's not only "whatcha say" but "how ya say it."

Welcoming Parents, Students, and Community Members

When anyone comes to your school, they must feel welcome. The climate of the front office should feel "warm" and inviting. The following are essential for creating this type of climate in any school:

- Smiling at parents, students, and visitors when they enter the front office

- Greeting them (e.g., "Good morning." "Good afternoon." "We'll be right with you.")

- Offer assistance (e.g., "What can I do for you?" "How can I help you, Mom?")

When the Phone Rings

Much like the front desk folks are the "face" of a school, they are often the "voice" as well! When people call, it is essential they are treated with respect and kindness—with a kind of "at your service" attitude. When your staff answer the phone, be sure they convey that attitude and use greetings such as:

- "Good morning! Central Neighborhood School, how may I assist you?"

- "It is a wonderful day at Central Neighborhood School! How may I assist you?"

Listen to Parents When They Are Upset

Effective customer service starts by listening to what parents say about their needs, wants, or concerns. If you can provide complete and honest answers to their questions, you strengthen trust and further establish your school's standing with them. Oftentimes the honest answer might be, "I'm not sure." This is OK—nobody has all the answers! Being open and honest increases the likelihood the parents will want to listen to school representatives in the future. In addition, parents are rarely upset with your front desk folks, so help them to avoid taking it personally! This can be difficult, but it's achievable and worth the effort. When it comes to issues related to people's children, emotions can mount. Oftentimes the issue can be directly related to miscommunication between the home and the school. School personnel should be a model for all. When parents are upset, front office folks may try:

Doing the following:

- Bringing their volume down as the parent's volume goes up

- Using facial expressions and vocal tones that express concern

Saying the following:

- "Mom, you look upset. Let me find somebody who can help you with this."

- "Is there anything I can do to help you?"

- "While I don't have the answer, I can contact _____ to find out."

- "Dad, please know I am doing my best to help you."

If parents are using inappropriate language or are highly escalated, staff might say:

- "Let me see if I can get one of our administrators to help you immediately."

All school personnel (administrators, too!) should avoid saying the following:

- "Calm down."

- "If you would just give me a minute."

Responses of this nature are likely to have the opposite of the intended effect, as parents will usually escalate if they are told this ... and we don't blame them!

Be Flexible

All districts and schools have policies and procedures that govern the day-to-day routines. These are meant to create order and safety at the school site. However, there are times when judgment must be used. Flexibility (as opposed to hyper-rigid adherence to policy and procedure) strengthens relationships and fosters loyalty. If your front office personnel are unsure, tell them they should seek out an administrator. Here are examples of exceptional and reasonable cases where flexibility might be justified:

- School begins at 8:45 a.m. A parent drops a student off at 8:46 a.m. and does not come into the school to sign the student in because the parent is injured.

- A parent has an emergency and must check the child out at 2:50 p.m. before the 3:10 p.m. pick-up policy.

Provide Quick Responses

When front office personnel are unable to provide a quick response to a parent, the parent may become frustrated ... even though the front office staff is typically not to blame! Schools are large and complex systems; sometimes, "things" take time. As a parent, this can be frustrating. Think about it. Have you ever been on hold or waiting for a business to return your call only to become agitated from lack of a timely response? This can give the impression that the business does not value you.

Parents are likely to feel the same way. When front office personnel cannot respond quickly, they should inform the parent and use an empathy statement. They might try saying something along the lines of:

- "I'm sorry it's taking so long. I know it must be frustrating. Please know we are working on it."

- "I would be concerned as well. Let me see how I can help."

Be Humble and Apologize When Mistakes Happen

It might not have been the front office personnel's fault (or yours). But does that matter? If the parent has suffered or is unhappy because of something that happened at your school, that's a reason to apologize—in a meaningful way. Any school personnel (including you!) should tell them honestly— as a school representative—that they are sorry and will do their best to ensure it doesn't happen again. That's a powerful symbolic gesture that you and your personnel have the highest standards and consider yourselves accountable for service and support.

Frequently Asked Questions (FAQs) and Responses

Finally, at your school, it might be a good idea to create a FAQs sheet that can be posted in the front office or distributed to parents as needed. This sheet might have common questions such as the following, with responses that fit the context of your school:

1. Can I walk my child to class?
2. Can I pick up work for my child?
3. Can I observe my child in class?
4. Can I see the principal now?
5. Can I pick up my student before dismissal?
6. Why do I always have to provide my ID?
7. Can I change my child's transportation?
8. How do I get my child tested?
9. Can I speak to the teacher now?
10. Can you give my child medication?

Front office personnel are an extremely valuable part of your school. They can often foster a strong connection between the home and the school. Though it's often said, "Don't judge a book by its cover," human nature tends to do exactly that. Invest in your front office folks, as they are the "cover" of your school.

Train front office personnel. Help them by posting visual aids around the front office as reminders (e.g., smiley faces or greeting reminders by the phone). And when you see them effectively applying these strategies, recognize them. Provide them with reinforcing feedback. Treat them as if they are your customers. It's been our experience that the most effective leaders share a concern and seek to bring out the best in all stakeholders. Helping to bring out the best in your front desk staff can be an immediate Quick Win.

Quick Takeaways:

- Front office personnel are valuable to your school. They can often foster a strong connection between the home and the school.
- Positive interactions with the front office staff strengthen relationships with the community.
- The climate of the front office should feel warm and inviting.
- Flexibility strengthens relationships and fosters loyalty.
- When people call, treat them with respect and kindness, a kind of "at your service" attitude.

- Effective customer service starts by listening to what parents say about their needs, wants, or concerns.

- If a parent is unhappy because of something that happened at your school, apologize.

Sustain It:

- Observe the customer service practices in your school. Are there areas in your school that may benefit from customer service training?

- If your school doesn't already have one, consider creating a fact sheet for frequently asked questions for parents.

CHAPTER 12:

Improving Teacher Evaluations

Teacher turnover is a national plague hurting our children, especially those in high-poverty schools and in classrooms serving students with disabilities. Some reports suggest teacher turnover costs 2.2 billion dollars annually, and others have projected a teacher shortage of 316,000 by 2025 (Sutcher et al., 2016). Getting through the first year has not been easy for teachers, who can be so traumatized they leave the field altogether. Although data on new-teacher attrition vary, studies have found that nearly 46% of new teachers quit within their first 5 years (Ingersoll et al., 2018). Some research indicated that almost 70% of teachers leave schools serving low-income students and schools where 25% or more of the population are students of color (Carver-Thomas & Darling-Hammond, 2017). And this turnover isn't only in teachers.

Turnover rates for principals are scary, especially given that principals have been found to impact student achievement by up to 25% (Seashore Louis et al., 2010). Research shows that principal attrition ranges from 15% to 30% each year, with especially high turnover rates in schools serving more low-income, minority, and low-achieving students (Levin & Bradley, 2019). As the research suggests, teachers and leaders are coming into the field unprepared to meet the demands of the classroom and school. A big problem is that teacher and leader preparation programs are primarily rooted in theory, with little practice and oftentimes zero coaching. Check out the research regarding the generalization of skills in the classroom when a teacher is only taught educational theory. It's dismal, but it makes sense! *(See Figure 12.1 on the following page.)*

Unfortunately, teacher and principal attrition are often at the expense of their mental health, career, the taxpayers, and most importantly, our students' success and future livelihoods. What's troubling to us is that the blame is pointed at these folks instead of on the root cause, and evaluations are frequently used as the proverbial smoking gun.

Professional Development Elements

- **Knowledge Level**
  Estimated percentage of participants understanding content

- **Skill Attainment**
  Estimated percentage of participants demonstrating proficiency in the instructional practices

- **Transfer to Practice**
  Estimated percentage of participants regularly implementing instructional practices in the classroom

THEORY
(e.g., presenter explains content—what it is, why it is important and how to teach it)

DEMONSTRATION
(e.g., presenter models instructional practices)

PRACTICE
(e.g., participants implement instructional practices during the session[s])

COACHING
(e.g., participants receive ongoing support and guidance when they return to the classroom)

FIGURE 12.1: Student achievement through staff development. Adapted from Joyce and Showers (2002).

Some suggest leaders and teachers aren't putting in enough effort to learn, but those making that suggestion aren't out there in the trenches.

Learning under stressful conditions is extremely challenging. We must progressively set people up for success. We find it ironic that higher education does a poor job of educating our own. Too many teachers entering the field of education do not possess the prerequisite skills for teaching (through no fault of their own). This lack of preparedness places school districts and leaders in tough positions as feedback and limited professional development offered are often necessarily focused on developing fundamental skills rather than on deepening pedagogy. And because there is very little of the science of human behavior taught to district and school leaders, performance evaluations, in some cases, inadvertently become a weapon of destruction rather than a tool for growth.

Performance evaluations are considered a necessary evil by many. Often dreaded by teachers and school leaders alike, many evaluation systems typically seem to do more harm than good despite the recommendation by researchers and professionals that evaluation systems should be used to help teachers instruct better (Marzano & Toth, 2013).

Don't be mad at researchers like Marzano, whose name is paired with poorly conceived evaluation processes. His meta-analysis is fantastic. It lists instructional practices that yield the highest impact on student achievement. Unfortunately, evaluation systems are often bastardizations of existing research never intended to be used as evaluations. Having a list of the best instructional practices is great. The issue lies in building fluency in our teachers and using an evaluation system as a feedback tool that helps, not hurts.

If it were up to us, we'd trash teacher evaluations. We'd then link up with leaders in the field of performance management to develop a fair and simple system rooted in behavioral science and focused on improving teacher performance, not evaluating it, much as we've outlined in this book. As that likely won't happen soon, we will plug on. If you suspect issues with your teacher evaluation system, keep reading. We have found a Quick Win that might be helpful.

Tip 1: Simplify the Process

While there are elements of teacher evaluation common to performance improvement strategies (i.e., pinpointed instructional behaviors, metrics, feedback), there are a couple of issues that plague many evaluation systems. Beyond the subjectivity and measurement errors commonly associated with evaluation, one typical issue is the response effort required by administrators. In other words, the amount of time and effort it takes for administrators to conduct and record observations hampers the ability of administrators to provide adequate levels of observation and feedback. Because of the effort involved, evaluations quickly fall into a compliance measure akin to simply "checking it off the list" as school leaders scramble to avoid scrutiny from the district.

Where the effort required of an evaluation process may be manageable in some schools, it can be a struggle in others within the same district—*especially* in high-poverty schools. We've worked across middle-class and high-poverty schools for years. Trust us, the demands in high-poverty schools far outweigh those with a more affluent population.

Those who think differently have probably never spent extended time in a turnaround school within a poor community. These conditions put a large strain on every aspect of education, including the evaluation process. The struggle is real and often shapes evaluations into an ineffective measure of compliance that drains the time of leaders who would likely be more effective in leading than evaluating!

The field of education should take a page out of the OBM field and the business world, where there has been a focus on process improvement strategies for years. There are many books dedicated to the topic of making processes efficient because of the financial burden imposed by lengthy and redundant processes. The bottom line is this: Before evaluations can be effective, they must be relatively easy to implement within the school context.

Tip 2: Make Scales Work

Many school districts are using an evaluation scale that places school leaders in challenging situations as it doesn't allow them to recognize incremental growth. These scales might look like this:

Rating	Innovating	Applying	Growing	Beginning	Not Using
Scale	4	3	2	1	0

FIGURE 12.2: Common evaluation scale.

Using the above scale as an example, a teacher who was rated a two and made some improvement would be rated a two again if they did not meet the criteria for applying the skill. Can you see the quandary here? Rating the teacher at level two might hurt their relationship with the evaluator and deflate morale. However, providing the teacher a score of three gives inaccurate feedback and can hamper growth. Rather than cite researchers in the behavioral science field or suggest you go out and buy another book, we are going right to the horse's mouth regarding the use of scales for improving performance. Marzano and Toth (2013) suggest the following regarding scales:

> "*Make concrete cut-points in the scale .... Although our scale for measuring teachers' levels of competence on the 41 strategies has five levels ... there are probably many more*" (p. 66).

Take a look at this simple example and compare it to the standard above:

Rating	Innovating	Applying	Growing	Beginning	Not Using
Scale	10 9	8 7 6	5 4 3	2 1	0

FIGURE 12.3: Behaviorally anchored rating scale.

A scale like this allows leaders to acknowledge and reinforce incremental growth of instructional practices (Marzano & Toth, 2013), a process that you now know as shaping. Now mind you, you can't just throw more numbers in the scale and expect this to work. Just as the simpler scale must be behaviorally anchored, so must each "nuanced gradation." Creating an evaluation system takes some work up front, but the payoff would be tremendous. And we would recommend that school districts work with their teacher unions to anchor this. But even if you just started by expanding the scale and progressively anchoring it as you move throughout the school year, you can still use your judgment to improve. For example, in the past, when you knew a teacher had made progress in "Growing," but they weren't quite performing at the "Applying" level, you can now move them up the scale under the "Growing" classification to reinforce progress!

Rating	Innovating		Applying			Growing			Beginning		Not Using
Scale	13	12	11	10	9	8	7	6	5	4	0

FIGURE 12.4: Behaviorally anchored rating scale adjusted for acceptance.

Now take a look at this scale. You have likely noticed and wondered about this: The scale ranges from 4 through 13. Well, take a moment to think about it. When it comes to these types of evaluation ratings, we tend to operate on a 10-point scale and think in percentages: 90%–100% is great, 80%–90% is good, 70%–80% is OK, 60%–70% is not so good, and below 60% is bad. This type of evaluation is buried deep in our psyche.

Let's look at a teacher being rated on a traditional 10-point scale as illustrated in Figure 12.3. If she had improved performance in some area that moved her from "Growing" to "Applying," on a scale ranging from 1–10, she would move from a 5 to a 6. Now while that is "Applying," in her mind, 6 is "not so good" as it's equated to the 60% marker in our heads.

Take that same rating and apply it to the 4 through 13 scale illustrated in Figure 12.4. She now moves from an 8 to a 9 and 9 is great because it's associated with 90%. Even though it's the same rating, it's experienced in a different light and therefore is more likely to be accepted. Besides, when arranged this way, "Applying" is the goal. We can't expect all or even most teachers to be "Innovating"—that's rare. So, if somebody is marked as "Innovating," it should be seen as going above and beyond and should be represented on the scale as such!

Final Thoughts on Evaluations

Your experience may not lead you to agree with the issues we've highlighted or to be inclined to try the modifications to traditional observation rating scales we've provided. And that's OK. If you are in a district where the evaluation process works well and is perceived positively by teachers and leaders, keep doing what you are doing.

But if you are not, we hope this Quick Win helps you and your teachers get out of the quicksand associated with traditional performance evaluations.

Quick Takeaways:

- Some reports suggest teacher turnover costs 2.2 billion dollars annually, and others have projected a teacher shortage of 316,000 by 2025.

- Nearly half of new teachers quit within their first 5 years. This number is higher for teachers working in schools serving a low-income population and populations with a high percentage of students of color.

- School administrators are leaving the field. Leadership attrition ranges from 15% to 30% each year, with especially high turnover rates in schools serving more low-income, minority, and low-achieving students.

- Skills taught in teacher preparation programs need to prepare educators to meet the demands of the classroom as a lack of preparedness places school districts and leaders in tough positions as feedback and limited professional development offered are often necessarily focused on developing fundamental skills rather than on deepening pedagogy.

- Leaders should focus on building fluency in teachers and using an evaluation system as feedback.

- Subjectivity, measurement errors, and response effort plague teacher evaluations. The time and effort it takes for administrators to conduct and record observations is a barrier to providing teachers with adequate feedback on their performance.

- Behaviorally anchored scales are relatively easy to implement within the school context and evaluate teachers on a scale that reinforces and acknowledges incremental growth of instructional practices.

Sustain It:

- Does your current teacher evaluations system work for your teachers? How might you find out? Identifying a Quick Win, how might you improve the process if it's not working?

- How often are teacher evaluations conducted? What does your teacher evaluations system look like? Consider ways you might improve your current teacher evaluation scale and system.

- How might you behaviorally anchor the ratings? What specific behaviors can you identify that you can shape and reinforce?

- How often are teachers being evaluated? Consider the benefit of more frequent and shorter teacher evaluations.

CHAPTER 13:

Involving Stakeholders in Goal Selection

Principal Daniels used input from faculty and staff to set goals to improve three areas: 1) arrival, 2) cafeteria, and 3) the front office. Involving the stakeholders demonstrated respect, included them in the decision-making process, and offered choices—a powerful reinforcer. Unfortunately, in too many schools, goal setting is approached as a top-down one-person show with major drawbacks. Avoid simply imposing goals on people. The process is already stalling if your faculty and staff do not feel involved. To create enthusiasm and commitment, involve your staff in goal setting by seeking input from them. This can be done individually or in small or large groups. Although the personal touch is always best, using surveys is an efficient strategy for gaining input in a way that allows you to recognize patterns easily. Involving your staff in selecting goals is one of your first Quick Wins.

Involving Staff

Obviously, if you are reading this, it is because you know that school improvement can be tough. Kotter (1996) suggests establishing a sense of urgency is crucial to gaining cooperation in organizational change. In the behavioral world, we might call this "sense of urgency" a motivating operation (MO). An MO, as known in the science of human behavior, is an environmental variable with a value- and behavior-altering effect. More simply, it creates a "want" that increases the likelihood that people will engage in the required behaviors to achieve a goal and less in behaviors that move away from a goal. For example, when you are thirsty, water is valuable at that moment and increases the likelihood that you'll engage in behavior to get water. On the other hand, water is not as valued if you're not thirsty; therefore, you're less likely to engage in certain behaviors to get it.

Without a sense of urgency, which might be characterized as "thirst" in the water example, successful teamwork is unlikely as it becomes challenging to develop a team with enough collaborative effort that will move them toward the school-improvement goals and school leader's vision (Kotter, 1996). But even with a sense of urgency solidly in place, some resistors will tend to "dig in" more because change is not palatable for them. Because change requires people to behave differently, it makes sense that human behavior is the biggest factor in a change failure. When school leaders are ineffective in changing the behaviors of their leadership team, faculty, staff, and students, resistance is compounded, and the initiative is more likely to be abandoned.

One common creation of resistors is what Daniels (2016) calls the principle of supply push. This is where people are pushed into training, pushed into engaging in initiatives, pushed into giving up control, and pushed into having to take on additional job responsibilities (Daniels, 2016). In contrast, Daniels recommends a demand-pull model whereby reinforcement is used to create a situation where a team desires to move forward with the change, wants to receive more training, and wants to move to the next stage in the transition process. By utilizing reinforcement to move behavior through the demand-pull model, resistance is less likely to occur as acceptance and change become highly reinforcing.

And what is a simple leadership strategy for doing this? You guessed it! Involving stakeholders in the planning initiative, goal setting, and decision-making. By engaging faculty, staff, and even students in the process, each can provide input and serve as a potentially rich source of knowledge that might add great value to the initiative. In addition, this often improves the relationship between leadership, faculty and staff, and even students. Moreover, this approach fosters a sense of teamwork that often manifests itself as self-directed and goal-oriented behavior because faculty and staff (and sometimes students) feel part of the process and are more willing to put forth the effort required to make the change work.

As such, IMPACT Goals can be extremely powerful for engaging people, including yourself, in the movement toward the eventual attainment of desired outcomes. When faculty and staff are engaged, they:

- Use terms such as "we" instead of "you" or "them"
- Regularly fly the school's colors within and outside of the school setting
- Are connected with and participate in activities with faculty and staff outside of the normal school day
- Are more concerned with performance and accomplishments of their students, themselves, and the school, than they are with hours worked
- Offer to support others, even outside of their department
- Regularly seek out solutions to problems as opposed to problems with solutions
- Seek to better themselves in a way that also benefits the school and the students

When you inspire and involve educators in goal setting, they are more likely to feel invested. Consequently, their day-to-day behaviors are driven by the accomplishments produced by themselves ... and the students. In other words, their behaviors are getting in touch with naturally occurring positive reinforcement as they see themselves and the students moving toward individual and collective goals that benefit the school.

3+3+60=Trust

When Principal Daniels first took over the school, he knew many things needed to be done. He also knew that getting those things done would require the collective effort of everybody at the school, so he needed buy-in. While he could tell those involved at the school everything they needed and should have been doing in the first place, that would only produce short-term outcomes—and at the cost of buy-in, morale, sustainability, retention, and student success. So rather than push faculty and staff to do things more, less, or differently, he knew he needed to build trust and buy-in with them as soon as possible. He needed a Quick Win. So here is what he did.

In the first meeting with his new staff, Principal Daniels said, "*Give me three things you **don't** want me to change (keepers) and three things you **do** want me to change (fixes).*" And he did this in his first 60 minutes with them. What did it build? *Trust*. Thus, the magic formula: *3+3+60=Trust*

Some of the answers surprised Principal Daniels, but others did not. The "keepers" gave great insight into what the staff deeply valued, such as customs, rituals, and celebrations held near and dear. As Principal Daniels was fond of saying, "Don't mess with these, or you'll unsettle the masses." The "fixes" were things the faculty and staff perceived as needing immediate attention. Many were simple managerial behaviors, such as being more visible around campus. Throughout the 60 minutes, the team charted all the responses and reached a consensus by listing "three keepers and three fixes" as immediate goals to focus on. Principal Daniels utilized the 3+3+60=Trust strategy to initiate Quick Wins that turned around three underperforming schools within 7 years.

The 3+3+60=Trust strategy is intended for those stepping into a new leadership role in a new school or department. As such, you only get one shot at it at the very beginning of the relationship. If you get it right, everyone wins as they experience huge benefits!

Because he was devoting his time to the fixes, the faculty and staff immediately began to trust Principal Daniels, as he was attentive to their stated needs. The "fixes" were taking place while Principal Daniels celebrated the "keepers," and in doing so, he quickly established that he valued what his team held as important for *them* and *their* school. *Their voices* were heard, and the new guy wasn't barging in to change and invalidate everything they had. If you use the 3+3+60=Trust strategy, make sure you spend the first semester 100% committed to addressing the six items while constantly scanning the landscape for additional Quick Wins. And don't move in on the big ones yet!

If you implement this simple 3+3+60=Trust strategy just right, you will likely become the best thing since spring break in the eyes of your faculty and staff. You will be accepted, you will have earned their trust, and now any big changes you want to implement in the second semester or in Year Two will be easier mountains to climb.

Quick Takeaways:

- Involve stakeholders in the planning initiative, goal setting, and decision-making. By engaging faculty, staff, and even students in the process, each stakeholder group can provide input and serve as a rich source of knowledge that adds great value to the initiative.

- IMPACT Goals can be extremely powerful for engaging people toward attaining desired outcomes.

- When educators are involved in goal setting, they are more likely to feel invested.

- The 3+3+60=Trust strategy is the school leader asking faculty and staff three things they *don't* want the leader to change (keepers) and three things these stakeholders *do* want the leader to change (fixes). This strategy is implemented within the first 60 minutes of the meeting with the group.

- The 3+3+60=Trust strategy is intended for those stepping into a new leadership role in a new school or department. This is the first impression and an opportunity for building rapport with stakeholders. There is only one chance to get it right.

Sustain It:

- If you are a new leader, how might you incorporate the 3+3+60=Trust strategy when first meeting your team? What would be your next steps after gathering information and data from the stakeholders?

- If you are a leader looking for Quick Wins, how might you use the 3+3+60=Trust strategy to build trust and rapport with your team if you need to do some things more, less, or differently? What might the implementation of this strategy look like for you? What would be your next steps after engaging your team?

CHAPTER 14:

The Leadership Mirror

Telling school leaders to be better or pointing the finger at them only increases the attrition rate. Unfortunately, this is an approach employed by district leaders who do not understand the fundamental principles of human behavior. Districts would be best served by focusing greater energy on developing and coaching school leaders to bring out their best so they can bring out the best in others. They need help! And if you are a school leader reading this, share this chapter with your district leaders, as this is a Quick Win for you and them.

Though research on school leadership has underscored the importance of leadership preparation and development for school district leaders (Rebore, 2012), many leadership development and personal growth programs exist solely as compliance measures rather than powerful processes with the potential to benefit every student and staff within a district. This is especially unfortunate as many school leaders report that their college and pre-service programs did not prepare them for the demands of the position (Grissom & Harrington, 2010).

Leadership programs likely will need to rethink their preparation curriculum. Until then, it is clear that many school leaders need to be given greater support or need to find different ways to deepen their skill set. As school districts are often stretched thin, it is necessary to employ efficient strategies that can greatly impact performance and student achievement.

Sometimes there appears to be a disconnect between many leaders' self-perception and the perception of their followers in any industry. This includes district, school, and classroom leaders in education. Having an objective perception of oneself is a challenging endeavor. Some leaders may see themselves as eagles soaring high, with a bird's-eye view of progress toward a school's vision, mission, and goals. However, staff may have a different vision. From their perspective, if the leader walks like a duck ... and talks like a duck ... then the leader must be a duck!

In other words, the image reflected in the mirror may be different from what your staff sees. This may only be their perception; not rooted in reality. But as the old cliché goes, "Perception is reality." It is more common than you think for a school leader's intention to be mismatched with how teachers and staff view and receive their messages.

Unfortunately, people do not judge school leaders by their intentions but by their impact. For this reason, you *must* have a way to measure your impact on others beyond end-of-year student achievement scores. If schools and districts measure your impact only on academic achievement *results*, they may miss your *full impact* ... at the expense of students, staff, and greater leadership development.

As we've stated in earlier chapters, if you are a school leader, you *must* receive feedback on your leadership performance to know what you are doing well and where you can focus on growth. It is also a way to discover if the staff's perceptions are not aligned with the reality of your intentions. You can use these data to quickly exercise damage control and reshape perceptions through well-timed and effective communication. This is a Quick Win! And this is exactly what Principal Daniels did when he put out a weekly survey asking five simple questions that helped him initiate his Quick Wins and keep them going.

Developing Leaders Through Measurement

Whatever approach a school district decides to use for leadership development (and we hope it employs real behavioral science!), they *must* have a system for measuring leadership effectiveness as a tool for providing feedback and coaching to school leaders. As there is a good chance they don't, the 360-degree feedback process (commonly used in the business world) is a simple, cost-effective instrument you can use to examine and grow, using data based on the perceptions of your followers and others.

Also called multisource or multi-rater feedback, a 360-degree instrument can gather feedback from people who commonly interact with you and other leaders. This might include a variety of staff including superintendents, assistant superintendents, directors, coordinators, teachers, paraprofessionals, and maintenance, as well as parents and students.

The 360-degree feedback process is kind of like standing in front of a fitting room mirror as it allows leaders to take a look at the effectiveness of their leadership from different perspectives. Analysis of the feedback can be used as a formative assessment to guide your leadership development or that of anybody on your team. For any district leaders who may be reading this, it is essential to remember this type of measurement and feedback should be strategically employed to help school leaders grow, not used as a hammer or other tool to demonstrate to the leader that they are not measuring up (Alimo-Metcalfe, 1998; Edwards, 1996).

Thus, it is critical for senior district leadership to stress to all involved in the supervision and coaching of school leaders that the 360-degree feedback tool

FIGURE 14.1: *360-degree feedback serves as a formative assessment to guide leadership.*

is not an evaluation tool for hiring or firing principals but rather a powerful opportunity for leadership development (Moore, 2009). In fact, those tasked with coaching leadership should also be provided some measurement and feedback related to their coaching effectiveness. When used correctly, it can really help leaders help themselves so that they can better help others.

Essential Questions to Include in Every School Leader's 360-Degree Feedback

There are various 360-degree feedback tools on the market. Whichever you choose, we recommend including evaluations of the following statements as part of any measurement tool for assessing and helping leaders grow:

1. My school leader provides clear expectations of my role and responsibilities toward the school's success.

2. My school leader supports me by providing the necessary resources to make things happen.

3. My school leader enables my professional growth through professional development opportunities, coaching, and mentoring.

4. My school leader monitors my performance and gives me ongoing performance-based feedback, both positive and constructive.

5. My school leader consistently communicates with my peers and with me about the school's overall performance.

6. My school leader takes time to directly observe me in action—not to scrutinize but to optimize my performance.

7. My school leader provides ample reinforcement through recognition, positive feedback, and support when I need help.

Remember, the measure of a leader is ultimately found in the performance of his or her followers (Daniels & Daniels, 2007). So, school leaders need to receive feedback on which of their leadership behaviors to adjust or improve to effectively bring out the best in those around them.

If you are a school leader and want to assess and improve your professional growth, using 360-degree feedback tools can provide simple yet powerful leading indicators of your leadership. You don't need to wait for the district: Just do it in your school! Using this type of data to improve your leadership behaviors can be a Quick Win for improving staff performance, student achievement, and effectiveness as a leader. Like the fitting room mirror analogy, it should be used to look at leadership from the perspectives of different stakeholders. With these tools, you can measure and continually guide individual, classroom, and school growth, starting with the leader in the mirror.

Quick Takeaways:

• Telling school leaders what to do often fails in getting them to do it; moreover, it will not decrease the rate at which they leave the field.

• Understanding and using the principles of human behavior with a focus on developing and coaching school leaders will decrease their attrition rate and help them bring out the best in those they serve.

• Many school leaders report that their college and pre-service programs did not prepare them for the demands of the position. This is not helped by the current reality that too many of the district-driven professional development programs for school leaders exist only to meet compliance measures.

- Often there is a disconnect between many leaders' self-perception and the perception of their followers. Unfortunately, this includes school and district leaders.

- School leaders are not judged by their intentions but by their impact. Therefore, leaders must have a way to evaluate their leadership performance in real time, not at the end of the year when there is no opportunity for behavior change.

- School leaders can assess and improve their professional growth using 360-degree feedback tools. Don't wait for the district! This feedback tool can be used immediately within the school to collect data on the leader's performance. Improving leadership behaviors is often a Quick Win!

Sustain It:

- How often should you consider initiating feedback surveys?

- How might you get buy-in from teachers and staff to complete them?

- What should happen after you receive feedback on your leadership performance?

- How will you share this information?

- What would be the next steps?

- Who else might you solicit feedback from as a school leader?

- What are some other questions that may be critical to ask about how people are feeling about your leadership?

Final Thoughts

Hopefully, we've hammered this point home: School leaders are critical to staff performance and student achievement. Make no mistake, most school leaders want to make a positive difference. If you are reading this book, it is a sure indicator that you are one of those leaders. School leaders understand very well the ramifications of success—or lack thereof—to themselves, staff, families, students, and the community. We believe that good leaders help people, great leaders help people help themselves, and the best leaders help create more leaders. By taking a *Quick Wins* approach and developing leadership and staff skills as described in this book, success is a matter of "when," not "if."

Quick Wins aren't just about getting things going in the right direction; they are about sustaining them. Quick Wins are evidence-based approaches rooted in behavioral science for making change happen and last. Although Quick Wins are leader-led, they require the leader to involve the stakeholder in the change process. And the results of this change require a change of behavior—the behavior of folks doing something more, less, or differently to make the change happen. Recall that a good measure of leadership is people going above and beyond their daily tasks when no one is looking. How leaders get people to behave in ways that align with the school's vision, mission, and values requires modeling and reinforcement of valued behavior by the leadership. Effective communication is vital and has a profound, positive, and lasting effect on staff behavior and morale. If you want your initiatives to stick, involve your faculty and staff. When you have buy-in from your stakeholders, and they are involved in goal setting, they are more likely to feel invested. In addition, you will have created an environment as a leader for your team to be willing to take on more significant challenges in the future. This is the heart of Quick Wins.

Needless to say, we never claim that school improvement or turnaround is easy. However, taking a science-based, systematic approach to a turnaround results in better performance, better staff satisfaction, and more long-term results. While the science of human behavior that this book is grounded in doesn't provide all the solutions, it will help you to find the best ones. And in the case of Quick Wins, it will help you to find the best solutions quickly. Quick Wins bring out the best in students by bringing out the best in those who serve them.

Thanks for reading. We wish you well on your *Quick Wins!* journey!

—Paulie and Anika

Appendix A

IMPACT GOALS

INDIVIDUALIZED

The goal is relevant to the roles and responsibilities of the stakeholder(s).

The goal states specifically what the desired result is.

The goal is specific to the needs of the stakeholder(s).

MANAGEABLE

Staff have the knowledge and skills to reach this goal.

Resources have been provided to support those who need to implement the change (e.g., time, tools, authority, etc.).

The stakeholder(s) only focus on a few goals at a time.

POSITIVELY MOTIVATING

Stakeholders understand why they should engage in the change.

Stakeholders are involved in developing the goal.

Stakeholder(s) are motivated by the goal, or there is a plan for sustaining motivation.

Stakeholder(s) are involved in developing the goals.

ALIGNED

Specific behaviors and tasks required to achieve the goals have been identified.

The behaviors and tasks identified are specific to the roles and responsibilities of the stakeholder(s).

Achievement of this goal adds value to faculty, staff, and, ultimately, the students.

148

CONNECTED

Accomplishments have been identified that can be used as salient measures of progress.

The accomplishments are connected to the behaviors required to achieve them.

The goal is connected to the accomplishments required to achieve it.

TRACKABLE

There is a process for measuring behavior required to achieve accomplishments.

There is a process for measuring accomplishments required to achieve the goal.

There is a process for tracking stakeholder(s) perceptions.

Appendix B

QUICKWOC TEMPLATE

QuickWOC Part 1—Walkabout Observations

The QuickWOC is a collaborative approach for identifying Quick Wins for school turnaround efforts. The QuickWOC observation form is divided into seven domains that ask questions about the most visible common areas of the school. The areas identified are typically problematic during a school turnaround. For each question in the domain during the walkabout observation, rate it using the Likert scale.

Domain	Score				
ARRIVAL/DISMISSAL	1 Never	2 Rarely	3 Sometimes	4 Often	5 Always
1. Students walk during transitions.					
2. Students follow communication expectations (e.g., they speak at a conversational level).					
3. Students follow a designated route.					
4. Students transition directly to the designated area per the school's expectations.					
5. Staff attend their post on time.					
6. Staff stand in assigned areas.					
7. Staff greet the students and positively interact with them.					
8. Staff consistently correct misbehavior.					
9. When correcting misbehavior, staff use a calm and respectful manner.					

Domain	Score				
ARRIVAL/DISMISSAL	1 Never	2 Rarely	3 Sometimes	4 Often	5 Always
10. When a student runs, staff require the student to walk back to where they began running.					
11. Students transition safely to their transportation.					
12. Students move on and off the sidewalk in an orderly manner.					
13. Students have safe, designated areas to sit or stand while waiting for transportation.					
14. The front office staff smile at parents, students, and visitors when they enter the front office.					
15. The front office staff greet parents, students, and visitors (e.g., "Good morning," "We'll be right with you.").					
16. When answering the phone, the front office staff communicate in ways that convey respect, kindness, and an "at your service" attitude.					

Domain	Score				
HALLWAYS	1 Never	2 Rarely	3 Sometimes	4 Often	5 Always
1. Students walk during transitions.					
2. Students follow communication expectations (e.g., they speak at a conversational level).					
3. Students follow a designated route.					
4. Students transition directly to the designated area per the school's expectations.					
5. Staff attend their post on time.					
6. Staff stand in assigned areas.					

Domain	Score				
HALLWAYS	1 Never	2 Rarely	3 Sometimes	4 Often	5 Always
7. Staff constantly monitor their assigned area.					
8. Staff greet the students or provide random positive attention.					
9. Staff consistently correct misbehavior.					
10. When correcting misbehavior, staff use a calm and respectful manner.					
11. When a student runs, staff require the student to walk back to where they began running.					

Domain	Score				
CAFETERIA	1 Never	2 Rarely	3 Sometimes	4 Often	5 Always
1. Students transition through the line efficiently.					
2. It is easy for students to find seating (finding a seat creates little to no tension among students).					
3. Students pick up trash and deposit it in the correct containers.					
4. Students follow expectations when they have finished eating.					
5. Students face forward with their feet on the ground.					
6. Students talk only to the students at their table and do not yell across tables.					
7. Students ask permission or follow school expectations before leaving their seats or area.					
8. Staff stand at assigned posts.					
9. Staff actively scan their assigned areas.					
10. Staff track potential problems and intervene early.					

152

Domain	Score				
CAFETERIA	1 Never	2 Rarely	3 Sometimes	4 Often	5 Always
11. Staff greet the students and positively interact with them.					
12. Staff consistently correct misbehaviors such as students leaving their area without permission or yelling across tables.					
13. Staff provide more positive interactions than corrections.					
14. Staff follow through on warnings for repeated misbehavior.					
15. Staff refrain from grouping and speaking amongst themselves.					

Domain	Score				
PLAYGROUNDS/FIELDS	1 Never	2 Rarely	3 Sometimes	4 Often	5 Always
1. There are identified boundaries.					
2. The equipment is organized and easy to access.					
3. Students use the playground equipment safely.					
4. The equipment is clean and safe.					
5. Staff consistently monitor students.					
6. Staff refrain from grouping and speaking among themselves.					
7. Staff actively scan their assigned areas.					
8. Staff track potential problems and intervene early.					

Domain	Score				
BATHROOMS	1 Never	2 Rarely	3 Sometimes	4 Often	5 Always
1. There are identified boundaries.					
2. Students enter the bathrooms in reasonable numbers (i.e., only a few students in the bathroom at one time).					
3. Students use the facility for its intended purpose.					
4. Bathroom areas have procedures that ensure students will not congregate.					
5. Staff monitor the bathroom areas to check for safety and cleanliness.					

Domain	Score				
CLASSROOMS	1 Never	2 Rarely	3 Sometimes	4 Often	5 Always
1. Students respond in a well-behaved manner toward the teacher and other adults in the room.					
2. Students respect the materials and property in the classroom.					
3. Students respect their fellow students.					
4. Core subject areas receive uninterrupted blocks of time.					
5. Classrooms have established routines and procedures that include behavioral expectations for all activities and transitions.					

154

Domain	Score				
FACILITIES	1 Never	2 Rarely	3 Sometimes	4 Often	5 Always
1. The school façade or the school grounds appear to be in good condition.					
2. The inside of the building, including bathrooms, hallways, storage areas, and teacher workrooms, are in good condition.					
3. Classrooms have enough storage cabinets, space, etc., to maintain a clean and orderly environment for learning.					
4. Students and teachers access materials easily and quickly.					

QuickWOC Part 2—Other Sources

Additional Sources of Information	Observation Notes
STAFF	
1. What changes could be made easily and quickly that would make a difference to staff doing their daily work?	
2. Are there materials and resources that staff need?	
PARENTS	
3. What areas do parents think need to change quickly to improve the school environment and help their children learn?	
COMMUNITY	
4. Are there changes that could occur quickly and make a difference to the community and its perception of the school?	
OBSERVATION TEAM	
5. What are the most pervasive problems identified by the team?	
6. How do the team's observations align with comments from staff, parents, and the community?	

OF THESE PROBLEMS, WHICH ONES COULD BE MOST EASILY REMEDIED?

156

Appendix C

PERFORMANCE DIAGNOSTIC CHECKLIST TEMPLATE

Part 3—The Performance Diagnostic Checklist

Specify a behavior you need to improve based on Parts 1 and 2 of QuickWOC. Walk through the questions from the viewpoint of the person performing the behavior. Identify a solution for any "No" response; the solution may be a Quick Win.

Antecedents and Information	YES	NO
1. Is there a written description stating the clear expectation of the educator regarding a particular instructional/behavioral strategy?		
2. Has the educator received adequate instruction about what to do (e.g., instructions such as "I want you to do this and this before we leave today")?		
3. Has the educator received formal training on this instructional/behavioral strategy? If yes, check all applicable training methods. ☐ Instructions ☐ Demonstration ☐ Rehearsal		
4. Is there a task aid visible **while** completing the instructional/behavioral strategy in question (e.g., reminders to prompt the strategy correctly at the right time/duration)?		
5. Can the educator state the purpose of the instructional/behavioral strategy?		
6. Is the educator verbally, textually, or electronically reminded to use the instructional/behavioral strategy? If yes, how often? ☐ Hourly ☐ Daily ☐ Weekly ☐ Monthly By whom? Check all that apply: ☐ Peer ☐ Coach ☐ Administrator ☐ Other		

Antecedents and Information	YES	NO
7. Are there frequently updated, challenging, and attainable goals the educator is comfortable with about the instructional/ behavioral strategy?		
8. Is the educator "aware" of the school's mission?		

Equipment and Processes	YES	NO
9. If equipment is required, is it available and in good working order (e.g., computer, A/V, mic, etc.)?		
10. Are the equipment and environment optimally arranged in a physical sense (e.g., the arrangement of the students' desks)?		
11. Are larger processes performing well despite incorrect instructional/ behavioral strategies (e.g., routines and procedures)?		
12. Are these processes written out and arranged logically?		
13. Can the educator implement the instructional/behavioral strategy without any obstacles (e.g., interruption by the intercom)?		

Knowledge and Skills—Training	YES	NO
14. Can the educator tell you what they are supposed to be doing and how to do it?		
15. Can the educator physically/verbally precisely demonstrate the instructional/behavioral strategy?		
16. If the instructional/behavioral strategy needs to be completed quickly, can the educator perform it at the appropriate speed?		

Motivation	YES	NO
17. Are educators motivated based on the outcomes following the completion of the task?		
18. Do educators see the positive effects of implementing the instructional/behavioral strategy (e.g., increased student engagement, increased assessment data, decreased misbehavior)?		

Motivation	YES	NO

19. Do administrators monitor the educator's behavior related to the task? If yes, how often?

☐ Hourly ☐ Daily ☐ Weekly ☐ Monthly

20. Does the educator receive feedback about their performance? If yes, By whom?

_____

and How often?

☐ Hourly ☐ Daily ☐ Weekly ☐ Monthly

How long of a delay between observing the instructional/behavioral strategy and delivering feedback?

_____

Check all that apply:

Feedback Focus:

☐ Positive ☐ Constructive

Feedback Type:

☐ Written ☐ Verbal ☐ Graphed ☐ Other

21. Is the instructional/behavioral strategy easy to implement?

22. Do other instructional/behavioral strategies appear to take precedence over the targeted strategy?

Bibliography

Alimo-Metcalfe, B. (1998). 360 degree feedback and leadership development. *International Journal of Selection and Assessment, 6*(1), 35–44. https://doi.org/10.1111/1468-2389.00070

Austin, J. (2000). Performance analysis and performance diagnostics. In J. Austin & J. E. Carr (Eds.), *Handbook of applied behavior analysis* (pp. 321–349). Context Press.

Bailey, J. S., & Austin, J. (1996). Productivity in the workplace. In M. A. Mattaini & B. A. Thyer (Eds.), *Finding solutions to social problems: Behavioral strategies for change* (pp. 179–200). American Psychological Association. https://doi.org/10.1037/10217-007

Balcazar, F. E., Hopkins, B. L., & Suarez, Y. (1985-1986). A critical, objective review of performance feedback. *Journal of Organizational Behavior Management, 7*(3-4), 65–89. https://doi.org/10.1300/J075v07n03_05

Bandura, A. (1977). Social learning theory. In B. B. Wolman & L. R. Pomroy (Eds.), *International encyclopedia of psychiatry, psychology, psychoanalysis, and neurology* (Vol. 10). Van Nostrand Reinhold.

Bandura, A. (1986). The explanatory and predictive scope of self-efficacy theory. *Journal of Social and Clinical Psychology, 4*(3), 359–373. https://doi.org/10.1521/jscp.1986.4.3.359

Bandura, A. (1997). *Self-efficacy: The exercise of control.* W. H. Freeman.

Becker, J. D. & Grob, L. (2021, August). *The school principal and teacher retention.* Metropolitan Educational Research Consortium. https://scholarscompass.vcu.edu/merc_pubs/126

Bill, K., Bowsher, A., Malen, B., Rice, J. K., & Saltmarsh, J. E. (2022). Making matters worse? COVID-19 and teacher recruitment. *Phi Delta Kappan, 103*(6), 36–40. https://doi.org/10.1177/00317217221082808

Bronkhorst, L. H., Meijer, P. C., Koster, B., & Vermunt, J. D. (2014). Deliberate practice in teacher education. *European Journal of Teacher Education, 37*(1), 18–34. https://doi.org/10.1080/02619768.2013.825242

Cardichon, J., Darling-Hammond, L., Yang, M., Scott, C., Shields, P. M., & Burns, D. (2020, February 12). *Inequitable opportunity to learn: Student access to certified and experienced teachers.* Learning Policy Institute. https://learningpolicyinstitute.org/product/crdc-teacher-access-report

Carr, J. E., & Wilder, D. A. (2016). The Performance Diagnostic Checklist—Human Services: A correction. *Behavior Analysis in Practice, 9*(1), 63–63. https://doi.org/10.1007/s40617-015-0099-3

Carr, J. E., Wilder, D. A., Majdalany, L., Mathisen, D., & Strain, L. A. (2013). An assessment-based solution to a human-service employee performance problem: An initial evaluation of the Performance Diagnostic Checklist — Human Services. *Behavior Analysis in Practice, 6*(1), 16–32. https://doi.org/10.1007/BF03391789

Carver-Thomas, D., & Darling-Hammond, L. (2017, August 16). *Teacher turnover: Why it matters and what we can do about it.* Learning Policy Institute. https://doi.org/10.54300/454.278

Collins, J. C., & Porras, J. I. (1997). *Built to last: Successful habits of visionary companies* (1st ed.). Harper Business.

Cornish, E. (2004). *Futuring: The exploration of the future.* World Future Society.

Daniels, A. C. (2016). *Bringing out the best in people: How to apply the astonishing power of positive reinforcement* (3rd ed.). McGraw-Hill Education.

Daniels, A. C., & Bailey, J. S. (2014). *Performance management: Changing behavior that drives organizational effectiveness* (4th ed. rev). Performance Management Publications.

Daniels, A. C., & Daniels, J. E. (2006). *Performance management: Changing behavior that drives organizational effectiveness* (4th ed.). Performance Management Publications.

Daniels, A. C., & Daniels, J. E. (2007). *Measure of a leader: The legendary leadership formula for producing exceptional performers and outstanding results.* McGraw-Hill Education.

DiNovi, B., & Gavoni, P. (2021). *The 5 scientific laws of life & leadership: Behavioral karma.* Cranberry Press.

The Doing What Works Library. (n.d.) Quick Wins. Retrieved March 15, 2023, from https://dww-library-files.wested.org/library/4-quick-wins.html

Doran, G. T. (1981). There's a S.M.A.R.T. way to write management's goals and objectives. *Management Review, 70*(11), 35–36.

Eckert, S. A. (2013). What do teaching qualifications mean in urban schools? A mixed-methods study of teacher preparation and qualification. *Journal of Teacher Education, 64*(1), 75–89. https://doi.org/10.1177/0022487112460279

Edwards, J. R. (1996). An examination of competing versions of the person-environment fit approach to stress. *Academy of Management Journal, 39*(2), 292–339. https://doi.org/10.2307/256782

Ennis, R. P., Flemming, S. C., Michael, E. L., & Lee, E. O. (2020). Using a tiered approach to support early childhood educators' use of behavioral strategies. *Education and Treatment of Children, 43,* 265–277. https://doi.org/10.1007/s43494-020-00027-x

Gavoni, P., Edmonds, W. A., Kennedy, T. D., & Gollery, T. (2017). Data on the data: A method for improving the fidelity of office discipline referral completion. *The Journal of Teacher Action Research, 3*(2), 30–44. https://nsuworks.nova.edu/cps_facarticles/1804

Gavoni, P., & Weatherly, N. (2019). *Deliberate coaching: A toolbox for accelerating teacher performance.* Learning Sciences International.

Geller, E. S. (2003). Should organizational behavior management expand its content? *Journal of Organizational Behavior Management, 22*(2), 13–30. https://doi.org/10.1300/J075v22n02_03

Gilbert, T. F. (1978). *Human competence: Engineering worthy performance*. McGraw-Hill.

Gladwell, M. (2011). *Outliers: The story of success*. Back Bay Books.

Goman, C. K. (2011). *The silent language of leaders: How body language can help-or hurt-how you lead*. Jossey-Bass.

Gray, S. P., & Streshly, W. A. (2008). *From good schools to great schools: What their principals do well*. Corwin Press.

Grissom, J. A., & Harrington. J. R. (2010). Investing in administrator efficacy: An examination of professional development as a tool for enhancing principal effectiveness. *American Journal of Education, 116*(4), 583–612. https://doi.org/10.1086/653631

Hall, G. E., & Hord, S. M. (2011). *Implementing change: Patterns, principles, and potholes* (3rd ed.). Pearson.

Hayes, S. C, Strosahl, K. D., Bunting, K., Twohig, M, & Wilson, K. G. (2004). What is acceptance and commitment therapy? In S. C. Hayes & K. D. Strosahl (Eds.), *A practical guide to acceptance and commitment therapy*. Springer. https://doi.org/10.1007/978-0-387-23369-7_1

Herman, K. C., Hickmon-Rosa, J., & Reinke, W. M. (2018). Empirically derived profiles of teacher stress, burnout, self-efficacy, and coping and associated student outcomes. *Journal of Positive Behavior Interventions, 20*(2), 90–100. https://doi.org/10.1177/1098300717732066

Hersey, P., Blanchard, K. H., & Johnson, D. E. (2001). *Management of organizational behavior: Leading human resources* (8th ed.). Prentice Hall.

Horcones, L. (1983). Natural reinforcement in a Walden two community. *Revista Mexicana de Análisis de la Conducta, 9*(2), 131–143.

Joyce, B., & Showers, B. (2002). *Student achievement through staff development* (3rd ed.). Association for Supervision and Curriculum Development.

Ingersoll, R., Merrill, E., Stuckey, D., & Collins, G. (2018). *Seven trends: The transformation of the teaching force—updated October 2018*. CPRE Research Reports. Retrieved March 17, 2023, from https://repository.upenn.edu/cpre_researchreports/108

Kent, R. S. (1986). *25 steps to getting performance problems off your desk—and out of your life!* Dodd Mead.

Kirkpatrick, D. L., & Kirkpatrick, J. D. (2007). *Implementing the four levels: A practical guide for effective evaluation of training programs*. Berrett-Koehler.

Kotter, J. P. (1996). *Leading change*. Harvard Business School Press.

Kramer, A. D., Guillory, J. E., & Hancock, J. T. (2014). Experimental evidence of massive-scale emotional contagion through social networks. *Proceedings of the National Academy of Sciences, 111*(24), 8788-8790. https://doi.org/10.1073/pnas.1320040111

Krapfl, J. E., & Kruja, B. (2015). Leadership and culture. *Journal of Organizational Behavior Management, 35*(1–2), 28–43. https://doi.org/10.1080/01608061.2015.1031431

Laipple, J. (2012). *Rapid change: Immediate action for the impatient leader*. Performance Management Publications.

Lankford, H., Loeb, S., & Wyckoff, J. (2002). Teacher sorting and the plight of urban schools: A descriptive analysis. *Educational Evaluation and Policy Analysis, 24*(1), 37–62. https://doi.org/10.3102/01623737024001037

Latham, G. I. (1998). *Keys to classroom management.* P & T Ink.

Lattal, D. & Porritt, M. (2008). Translating the science of behavior analysis to the workplace: One company's 30-year effort. *Revista Mexicana de Psicología, 25*(1), 27–44. http://www.redalyc.org/articulo.oa?id=243016300002

Levin, S., & Bradley, K. (2019, March 19). *Understanding and addressing principal turnover: A review of the research.* National Association of Secondary School Principals/Learning Policy Institute.

Malott, M. E. (2003). *Paradox of organizational change: Engineering organizations with behavioral systems analysis.* Context Press.

Mager R. F., & Pipe P. (1970). *Analyzing performance problems or "You really oughta wanna".* Fearon Publishers.

Marinell, W. H., & Coca, V. M. (2013). *"Who stays and who leaves?" findings from a three-part study of teacher turnover in NYC Middle Schools.* Distributed by ERIC Clearinghouse.

Marzano, R. J., Marzano, J. S., & Pickering, D. J. (2009). *Classroom management that works: Research-based strategies for every teacher* (1st ed.). Pearson.

Marzano, R. & Toth, M. (2013). *Teacher evaluation that makes a difference: A new model for teacher growth and student achievement.* ASCD.

Marzano, R. J., & Waters, T. (2009). *District leadership that works: Striking the right balance.* Solution Tree Press.

Marzano, R. J., Waters, T., & McNulty, B. A. (2005). *School leadership that works: From research to results.* ASCD.

Moore, B. (2009). Improving the evaluation and feedback process for principals. *Principal, 88*(3), 38–41.

Owens, R. G., & Valesky, T. C. (2015). *Organizational behavior in education: Leadership and school reform* (11th ed.). Prentice Hall.

Parsons, M. B., Rollyson, J. H., & Reid, D. H. (2013). Teaching practitioners to conduct behavioral skills training: A pyramidal approach for training multiple human service staff. *Behavior Analysis in Practice, 6*(2), 4–16. https://doi.org/10.1007/BF03391798

Polk, K., Schoendorff, B., Webster, M., & Olaz, F. (2016). *The essential guide to the ACT matrix: A step-by-step approach to using the ACT matrix model in clinical practice.* Context Press.

Rebore, R. W. (2012). *The essentials of human resources administration in education.* Pearson.

Reid, D. H., Parsons, M. B., & Green, C. W. (2012). *The supervisor's guidebook: Evidence-based strategies for promoting work quality and enjoyment among human service staff.* Habilitative Management Consultants.

Rogers, C. R. (1956). Client-centered therapy: A current view. In F. Fromm-Reichmann & J. L. Moreno (Eds.) *Progress in psychotherapy* (pp. 199–209). Grune and Stratton.

Seashore, K., Leithwood, K., Wahlstrom, K., & Anderson, S. (2010). *Investigating the links to improved student learning: Final report of research findings.* The Wallace Foundation. https://hdl.handle.net/11299/140885

Seashore Louis, K., Dretzke, B., & Wahlstrom, K. (2010). How does leadership affect student achievement? Results from a national US survey. *School Effectiveness and School Improvement, 21*(3), 315–336. https://doi.org/10.1080/09243453.2010.486586

Sigurdsson, S. O., & Austin, J. (2006). Institutionalization and response maintenance in organizational behavior management. *Journal of Organizational Behavior Management, 26*(4), 41–77. https://doi.org/10.1300/J075v26n04_03

Sinek, S. (2009). *Start with why: How great leaders inspire everyone to take action.* Portfolio.

Sinek, S. [@simonsinek]. (2021, April 7). *It's better to go slow in the right direction than to go fast in the wrong direction* [Tweet]. Twitter. https://twitter.com/simonsinek/status/1379864312597078018

Skinner, B. F. (1984). The shame of American education. *American Psychologist, 39*(9), 947–954. https://doi.org/10.1037/0003-066X.39.9.947

Supovitz, J., Foley, E., & Mishook, J. (2012). In search of leading indicators in education. *Education Policy Analysis Archives, 20*, 19. https://doi.org/10.14507/epaa.v20n19.2012

Sutcher, L., Darling-Hammond, L., & Carver-Thomas, D. (2016). *A coming crisis in teaching? Teacher supply, demand, and shortages in the U.S.* Learning Policy Institute. https://doi.org/10.54300/247.242

Vroom, V. H., & Jago, A. G. (2007). The role of the situation in leadership. *American Psychologist, 62*(1), 17–24. https://doi.org/10.1037/0003-066X.62.1.17

About the Authors

Paul "Paulie" Gavoni, Edd, BCBA

Specializing in human performance, coaching, and organizational leadership, Dr. Paul "Paulie" Gavoni is a behavior scientist and educator who has worked across education and human services for almost 3 decades. Known for his authenticity and practical approaches, he has served the needs of children and adults through various leadership positions. He is passionate about applying Organizational Behavior Management (OBM), or the science of human behavior, to bring out the best in people. He strives to make a positive difference by establishing safe, productive, and engaging environments that bring out the best in faculty and staff so they can bring out the best in the learners they serve. He is an active board member of the Opioid Awareness Foundation and the World Behavior Analysis Day Alliance.

Dr. Gavoni is a *Wall Street Journal* and *USA Today* best-selling co-author of *The Scientific Laws of Life & Leadership: Behavioral Karma*, *Quick Wins! Accelerating School Transformation through Science, Engagement, and Leadership* (1st ed.); *Deliberate Coaching: A Toolbox for Accelerating Teacher Performance*; *QUICK Responses for Reducing Misbehavior and Suspensions: A Behavioral Toolbox for Classroom and School Leaders*; and *MMA Science: A Training, Coaching, and Belt Ranking Guide*. He is proud to introduce OBM and applied behavior analysis to worldwide audiences through his numerous publications.

Beyond his work in education and human services, Dr. Gavoni is also a former Golden Gloves Heavyweight Champion and a highly respected striking coach in combat sports. Coach "Paulie Gloves," as he is known in the mixed martial arts (MMA) community, has trained world champions and UFC vets using technologies rooted in the behavioral sciences. Coach Paulie has been featured in the books *Beast: Blood, Struggle, and Dreams at the Heart of Mixed Martial Arts, A Fighter's Way*, and the featured article "Ring to Cage: How Four Former Boxers Help Mold MMA's Finest." He has also written extensively for various online magazines such as *Scifighting, Last Word on Sports*, and *Bloody Elbow*, where his Fight Science series continues to bring behavioral science to MMA. Finally, Paulie was also a featured fighter in *FX*'s highest rated show at the time, *The Toughman*, and as an MMA coach in the Lifetime reality series *Leave it to Geege*.

Anika Costa, MSEd, BCBA

Analytical and hardworking, Anika is known for her practical yet detail-oriented approaches to organizing and successfully seeing projects through to the end. Passionate about instructional design and teaching, her meticulous approach to developing and delivering training using behavior-analytic technologies increases engagement and learning at an accelerated rate.

As a behavior analyst, professor, and former teacher in New York City Public Schools, Anika is equipped with a specialized skill set that has allowed her to effectively work with teachers and school leaders in classroom and school improvement efforts across the nation. A seasoned consultant and mentor, she is also passionate about applying principles of Organizational Behavior Management (OBM) during assessment, training, and coaching initiatives to support measurable performance improvement within the natural environment.

Anika is laser-focused on process improvement and the use of instructional design in professional development. She is dedicated to teaching others behavioral coaching skills aimed at bringing out the best in behavior technicians, behavior analysts, teachers, and school leaders so they can bring out the best in the learners they support. She is also the proud co-author of the best-selling book *QUICK Responses for Reducing Misbehavior and Suspensions: A Behavioral Toolbox for Classroom and School Leaders.*

KeyPress Publishing

We strive to provide individualized services and support to all our authors. Our team of experts is here to answer all your questions and produce your ideal products. We offer personal attention from the time you reach out, through the writing, submission, and review process, close partnerships with our design team to fulfill your visions, and our publishing expertise to help you publish, promote, and sell your book.

A Sample of KeyPress Publications:

www.KeyPressPublishing.com

Made in the USA
Las Vegas, NV
23 September 2023